UNQUENCHABLE Grace OF GOD

PETER LENGWE

All Scripture quotations are taken from the New King James Version® (NKJV).

Printed in the United States of America

ISBN:
Softcover: 978-1-972299-42-5
Hardback: 978-1-972299-43-2
eBook: 978-1-972299-41-8

For permission requests, visit and write to the publisher at:

Peter Lengwe | THE BREAD OF LIFE GLOBAL MINISTRIES

DEDICATION

To Jesus Christ—

the Lamb who was slain,

the Savior of sinners,

the Lord of glory—

whose grace found me, forgave me, and is still forming me.

And to every hungry soul who longs to walk in holiness without losing the wonder of mercy—

to the weary believer who needs strength,

to the brokenhearted who needs restoration,

to the tempted who needs help in time of need,

and to the remnant who desires to finish well—

This book is dedicated to you.

May the God of all grace perfect, establish, strengthen, and settle you—

until the day you stand in His presence with joy.

ABOUT THE AUTHOR

Peter Lengwe is a Christian author, Bible teacher, and the founder of The Bread of Life Global Ministries. With a deep reverence for Scripture and a burden to see believers rooted in truth, repentance, and holy devotion to Jesus Christ, Peter writes with one aim: to awaken hearts to the fear of the Lord and to the transforming power of God's Word.

Known for his deep, Scripture-rich, and theologically grounded style—often drawing from Hebrew and Greek word studies—Peter's writings call readers beyond religious tradition into living intimacy with Christ, steadfast faith, and uncompromising holiness. His books are written to strengthen the Church, provoke spiritual maturity, and stir a fresh hunger for the presence of God.

Peter is also the author of In the Beginning the Heavens and the Earth as Created (2022), When Silence Speaks Louder, The Act of Obedience and But God! just to mention a few and he continues to develop Bible-based teaching resources that equip believers to endure, grow, and finish well in these times.

The Bread of Life Global Ministries exists to proclaim Jesus Christ, disciple believers through the Scriptures, and point hearts to the saving and sustaining grace of God.

PREFACE

UNQUENCHABLE GRACE OF GOD

There are words in Scripture that we use so often that we can forget their weight. Grace is one of them. It is spoken in greetings and benedictions, sung in hymns, printed on wall décor, and quoted in sermons—yet many believers still struggle to explain what grace truly is, where it begins, how it works, and what it produces when it is received in truth.

Grace is not a religious slogan. Grace is not God lowering His standards. Grace is not permission to remain unchanged. And grace is certainly not a shallow comfort for a shallow Christianity. Grace is the holy, loving, sovereign initiative of God toward undeserving people—an initiative that does not merely forgive, but transforms; does not merely rescue, but trains; does not merely start the journey, but sustains the believer all the way to glory.

The verse that became the burning spark behind this book is simple, yet endless in depth:

In one sentence, the Holy Spirit reveals that grace is not only a concept—it has appeared. Grace stepped into history. Grace came clothed in flesh. Grace has a face and a name: Jesus Christ. And because grace has appeared, salvation is not earned by human effort, purchased by religious performance, or inherited through tradition. Salvation is received as a gift, flowing from the heart of God through the cross of Christ.

But as I studied the Scriptures, I began to see that the grace of God is not only saving grace—it is also sustaining grace, teaching grace, empowering grace, establishing grace, and even warning grace. It is unquenchable because it flows from the nature of God Himself—steadfast, faithful, merciful, and true. The same grace that causes the sun to rise and the rain to fall is the grace that calls sinners to repentance. The same grace that justifies the ungodly is the grace that empowers the believer to live godly in a crooked generation. And the same grace that welcomes us is the grace that keeps us—if we continue in faith, if we abide in Christ, and if we refuse the deception of a gospel without holiness.

This is why this book begins where all true biblical study should begin: with the Word itself. We will explore the meaning of grace from the language of Scripture—both Hebrew and Greek—so the reader can gain understanding "from the gate." My desire is not to impress the mind, but to awaken the spirit. Not merely to inform the believer, but to strengthen the believer. And not merely to comfort, but to convict us into the fear of the Lord and the love of truth.

You will find throughout these pages that grace has dimensions:

- Grace that sustains all creation—life, breath, provision, and restraint

- Grace that brings salvation through Christ Jesus alone

- Grace received by faith, apart from works

- Grace that justifies, establishes, strengthens, and perfects the believer

- Grace that teaches us to deny ungodliness and live soberly, righteously, and godly

- Grace that fuels obedience, endurance, ministry, healing, and spiritual warfare

- Grace that helps us obtain God's promises

- Grace that flows from the throne of God in "time of need"

- Grace that must be treasured, guarded, and not treated lightly

And yes—because Scripture is honest, this book will also address a teaching that has wounded many: the idea that a believer can live in willful sin, unbelief, or spiritual compromise and still claim eternal security as though grace cannot be resisted, and as though warnings in Scripture are merely symbolic. We will not build doctrine on emotion, tradition, or fear. We will open the Bible and let the Word speak. Grace is powerful—but it is not to be mocked. Grace is abundant—but it is not to be abused. Grace is free—but it is not cheap.

I write these pages with one prayer: that you would not only know about grace, but that you would stand in it, grow in it, and be established by it. That you would encounter the grace of God in such a living way that sin loses its charm, compromise loses its excuse, and Christ becomes more precious than every earthly desire. That you would come boldly to the throne of grace—not occasionally, but continually—and find mercy, cleansing, strength, and help.

If you are reading this and you feel far from God, I want you to know something from the start: the grace of God has appeared. It is reaching for you even now. And if you are reading this as a believer who has grown weary, pressured, or wounded, I want you to know this as well: His grace is sufficient. He has not brought you this far to leave you. He is able to restore, strengthen, and establish you.

May the Lord use this book as a trumpet and as a balm—calling the sleeping to wake, the drifting to return, the weary to rise, and the hungry to come and be filled.

"Grace to you and peace from God our Father and the Lord Jesus Christ." (Romans 1:7, NKJV)

Amen.

INTRODUCTION

Grace That Sustains the Believer—and Grace That Leads to Repentance

There is a grace that saves, and there is a grace that sustains. Many believers rejoice at the doorway of salvation—yet struggle in the hallway of endurance. They can testify that Christ forgave them, but they quietly wonder if God will keep them. They can speak of the cross, but they feel weak when temptation returns. They believe the gospel is true, yet their hearts grow tired under the pressure of life, trials, spiritual warfare, and the weight of their own humanity.

This is where the sustaining grace of God becomes more than doctrine—it becomes life.

The grace that sustains a believer is not merely God overlooking weakness; it is God supplying strength. It is not simply pardon; it is power. It is not only the forgiveness of sins; it is the ongoing ministry of Christ to the soul. Grace does not only pull a man out of the pit—grace teaches his feet how to walk on the narrow way. Grace does not only rescue from judgment—grace rescues from bondage. Grace does not only bring you into the Kingdom—grace keeps you faithful within it.

The Scripture does not speak of grace as a one-time encounter, but as a present realm in which the believer stands:

"Through whom also we have access by faith into this grace in which we stand..." (Romans 5:2, NKJV)

To stand in grace means to live under heaven's supply. It means Christ is not only your Savior from sin, but your Savior from sinking. It means the Lord does not merely demand holiness while watching from afar—He gives grace that trains the heart, renews the mind, strengthens the will, and establishes the soul. It is grace that holds you up when you feel you cannot hold on.

And yet, this same grace that sustains is also the grace that confronts.

This is where many misunderstand the heart of God. They imagine that conviction is condemnation, and they treat repentance as though it were a threat. But biblical repentance is not the voice of an angry God trying to destroy you; it is the voice of a holy Father trying to restore you. Repentance is not the opposite of grace—repentance is the fruit of grace. True grace does not make sin feel safe; it makes sin feel heavy. True grace does not create a comfortable distance from God; it draws the heart near with trembling and love. True grace does not whisper, "It's fine." True grace pleads, "Come home."

The apostle Paul reveals something that pierces the soul when he asks:

"Or do you despise the riches of His goodness, forbearance, and longsuffering, not knowing that the goodness of God leads you to repentance?" (Romans 2:4, NKJV)

This is one of the most tender truths in all Scripture: God's goodness leads. His kindness calls. His patience pulls. His mercy beckons. The Lord does not only correct the believer with His holiness—He draws the believer with His love. Grace sustains you when you are weak, and grace awakens you when you drift. Grace comforts you in suffering, and grace convicts you in compromise. Grace is the gentle hand that wipes tears—and the faithful hand that refuses to let you keep the knife of sin pressed against your own soul.

Some believers have tasted grace but have not yet learned to trust grace. They think God will sustain them only if they never stumble. But the gospel reveals a Savior who intercedes, a Shepherd who restores, and a High Priest who sympathizes:

"For we do not have a High Priest who cannot sympathize with our weaknesses..." (Hebrews 4:15, NKJV)

Grace is not given because you are strong; grace is given because He is faithful. And because He is faithful, grace does not excuse what is destroying you—it delivers you from it. It does not merely quiet the conscience; it cleanses it. It does not merely cover sin; it breaks its power. It does not only remove guilt; it produces godly sorrow that leads to life. When grace truly touches the heart, it does not create a casual Christianity. It creates a contrite spirit. It births a holy hatred for sin—not because the believer fears punishment, but because the believer has seen the cost of redemption and the beauty of the One who paid it.

There is a sorrow that is worldly—sorrow that regrets consequences but not sin. But there is a sorrow that is godly—sorrow that grieves because love has been wounded, because fellowship has been interrupted, because the Holy Spirit has been resisted. Godly sorrow is not despair; it is a doorway back to joy:

"For godly sorrow produces repentance leading to salvation, not to be regretted..." (2 Corinthians 7:10, NKJV)

This is what sustaining grace does. It keeps the believer from hardening. It keeps the heart tender. It keeps the conscience alive. It keeps the fear of the Lord burning while the love of God grows deeper. It teaches you to return quickly—before sin becomes a root, before compromise becomes a lifestyle, before distance becomes numbness.

Grace does not only sustain you when you are attacked from without; it sustains you when you are tempted from within. It gives you strength to resist. It gives you humility to confess. It gives you courage to cut off what feeds darkness. It gives you hope that restoration is real. It gives you a fresh hatred for what once captivated you, and a fresh hunger for what is eternal.

And if you have ever wondered whether you have exhausted God's patience—whether you have failed too many times, drifted too far, quenched the Spirit too deeply—hear this with reverence: grace is unquenchable, but the heart can become dull. That is why Scripture calls believers not only to receive grace, but to guard it, to continue in faith, and to pursue holiness. The grace that sustains you is not a license to wander— it is the strength to endure. It is not permission to remain unchanged—it is power to be transformed.

This book is written for the believer who desires more than a religious label. It is written for the soul that longs to be clean, stable, mature, and alive before God. It is written for the weary saint who needs strengthening, and for the compromised believer who needs awakening. It is written for anyone who wants to understand grace not as a soft word, but as a holy fire—gentle enough to heal, strong enough to deliver, faithful enough to restore, and severe enough to warn.

My prayer as you begin is simple: that you will not only learn about grace, but encounter it—so deeply that repentance becomes your refuge, holiness becomes your desire, and Jesus Christ becomes your treasure.

"For the grace of God that brings salvation has appeared to all men..."
(Titus 2:11, NKJV)

May that grace appear to you afresh—sustaining you, correcting you, and drawing you nearer to the heart of God.

Table of Contents

CHAPTER ONE:
WHAT IS GRACE? — THE HOLY FAVOR OF GOD THAT MUST NOT BE DESPISED

There are few words more beautiful on the lips of a believer than grace—and few words more dangerous when they are spoken without trembling.

Grace is not a decoration for Christian language. Grace is not a soft blanket to cover spiritual laziness. Grace is not the permission slip to live as we please while still claiming the name of Christ. Grace is holy. Grace is costly. Grace is the heartbeat of the gospel—and the very thing many have learned to take for granted.

Scripture does not present grace as something casual. It speaks of grace as a treasure, as a power, as a realm we stand in, and as a gift that can be received in vain if the heart becomes dull. The same Bible that proclaims grace also warns believers not to neglect it, not to fall short of it, not to insult it, and not to turn it into a cloak for sin.

"We then, as workers together with Him also plead with you not to receive the grace of God in vain." (2 Corinthians 6:1, NKJV)

That is not a warning to unbelievers. That is a pleading to believers. It is possible to receive grace on the lips but resist it in the life—sing about it, quote it, wear it, yet never submit to the God who gives it. Grace can be admired without being obeyed. And when that happens, the heart drifts into a frightening place: familiarity without fear.

This chapter begins where every solid foundation must begin—by returning to the meaning of grace in the languages through which God chose to give His Word. When you understand the weight of the word, you will better understand the weight of the calling.

The Hebrew Roots of Grace: Favor That Humble Hearts Find

In the Old Testament, one of the key words that carries the idea of grace is חֵן (ḥēn)—often translated favor. It is the picture of acceptance granted, kindness shown, goodwill given. It is not demanded; it is granted. It is not earned; it is bestowed.

This is why Scripture repeatedly uses the phrase "find favor" or "find grace" in someone's sight. It is not the language of wages. It is the language of mercy.

"But Noah found grace in the eyes of the LORD." (Genesis 6:8, NKJV)

Noah "found" grace while the earth was filled with violence and corruption. That single line reveals a pattern that appears repeatedly throughout Scripture: God's grace is often found by the one who fears Him, walks with Him, and refuses the spirit of the age.

Another Hebrew stream that runs alongside grace is חֶסֶד (ḥesed)— God's covenant lovingkindness, steadfast mercy, faithful love. Where ḥēn often highlights favor given, ḥesed emphasizes God's faithful mercy within relationship—His loyal love that keeps His covenant promises even when people are unfaithful.

Together, these reveal something vital: grace is not a light thing in Scripture. It is God's favor and mercy flowing from His holy character—toward the undeserving—so that He may redeem, preserve, and sanctify a people for Himself.

The Greek Revelation of Grace: "Charis" — Gift, Favor, and Divine Enablement

In the New Testament, the primary word for grace is χάρις (cháris). It carries the idea of favor freely given—a gift that cannot be purchased. Yet in the New Testament, grace is more than a "kind attitude." Grace is also divine action—God working within the believer.

Grace is how salvation comes, and grace is how the believer continues.

"For by grace you have been saved through faith…" (Ephesians 2:8, NKJV)

But grace does not end at salvation. Grace becomes the strength of sanctification, endurance, ministry, and victory over sin.

"And God is able to make all grace abound toward you, that you… may have an abundance for every good work." (2 Corinthians 9:8, NKJV)

Notice the language: grace abounds toward you so that you may abound in good work. Grace is not merely a covering— it is a supply.

This is why the apostles do not speak as though grace makes obedience optional. They speak as though grace makes obedience possible.

Grace Must Be Treasured—Because Grace Can Be Despised

Here is where the holy fear of the Lord must enter: the Bible teaches that grace can be despised.

Paul writes:

"Or do you despise the riches of His goodness, forbearance, and longsuffering, not knowing that the goodness of God leads you to repentance?" (Romans 2:4, NKJV)

You can despise grace without cursing God. You despise grace when you treat His patience as approval. You despise grace when you interpret His mercy as permission. You despise grace when you continue in what Christ died to destroy.

Grace is meant to lead you to repentance—not to make you comfortable in sin.

And the writer of Hebrews issues a warning that should put reverence in every true believer:

"Looking carefully lest anyone fall short of the grace of God..."
(Hebrews 12:15, NKJV)

Grace is not only something you receive; it is something you must not fall short of. This does not mean grace is weak—it means the heart can harden, and the soul can drift, and the conscience can become numb. When grace is treated as common, sin becomes normal. When sin becomes normal, the fear of God disappears. And when the fear of God disappears, deception comes like a flood.

Saving Grace Is Not Only Pardon—It Is Training

One of the clearest proofs that grace is not a license is found in Titus, the very passage that birthed this book:

"For the grace of God that brings salvation has appeared to all men, teaching us that, denying ungodliness and worldly lusts, we should live soberly, righteously, and godly in the present age..." (Titus 2:11–12, NKJV)

Grace teaches. Grace trains. Grace instructs the redeemed to deny ungodliness. If what we call "grace" does not teach us to forsake sin, then what we are calling grace is not the grace that appeared in Jesus Christ—it is a counterfeit comfort.

Yes, we are saved by grace. But we are not saved to remain the same. Grace saves us from wrath, but also from bondage. Grace pardons, but also purifies. Grace covers, but also cleanses. Grace justifies, but also sanctifies.

A Needed Warning: Grace Is Not a Cloak for Darkness

The early church faced the same deception we face today: people turning grace into permission for the flesh. Jude speaks plainly:

"For certain men have crept in unnoticed... ungodly men, who turn the grace of our God into lewdness..." (Jude 1:4, NKJV)

This is not new. The devil has always hated grace because grace destroys his claim over sinners. So, he twists grace. If he cannot stop you from hearing the gospel, he will try to poison the gospel—by teaching you that grace means God no longer cares about holiness.

But the God who gives grace is the God who is holy. And the grace that truly comes from Him produces reverence, humility, repentance, and a growing hatred for sin.

The Fear of the Lord Keeps Grace Precious

The greatest protection a believer has against abusing grace is not mere religious discipline—It is godly fear. Not the fear of condemnation for those who are in Christ, but the fear of grieving the Holy Spirit. The fear of resisting truth. The fear of hardening the heart. The fear of treating the blood of Jesus like something common.

Grace is free to you, but it was not free to Him. Grace came through wounds. Grace came through scourging. Grace came through the cross. And if Calvary does not teach the believer to tremble at sin, then something is deeply wrong in the soul.

The question is not only: Have I received grace?

The question is also: Have I honored grace?

Because grace is unquenchable, yet the conscience can be quenched. Grace is abundant, yet the heart can become dull. Grace is powerful, yet the believer can receive it "in vain" if he refuses to let it transform him.

A Call to the Reader: Do Not Take Grace for Granted

Beloved, if you are in Christ, grace has appeared to you. You are not reading these words by accident. The Spirit of God is calling you deeper—out of shallow Christianity, out of casual repentance, out of secret compromise, out of familiarity without fear.

Do not use grace to excuse what Jesus came to crucify.

Do not call Him Savior and refuse Him as Lord.

Do not claim the cross and cling to sin.

Do not boast in forgiveness while rejecting transformation.

Instead, come back to the throne. Come back to repentance. Come back to the fear of the Lord, which is clean and enduring. Come back to the grace that not only saves—but teaches, sustains, strengthens, and establishes.

Closing Scriptures for Meditation (NKJV)

- *"We... plead with you not to receive the grace of God in vain." (2 Corinthians 6:1)*

- *"The goodness of God leads you to repentance." (Romans 2:4)*

- *"Looking carefully lest anyone fall short of the grace of God." (Hebrews 12:15)*

- *"The grace of God... has appeared... teaching us... denying ungodliness..." (Titus 2:11–12)*

CHAPTER TWO:
GRACE OVER ALL CREATION — THE KINDNESS OF GOD THAT SUSTAINS THE WORLD AND LEAVES NO ONE WITHOUT WITNESS

Before grace ever rescued you, grace was already surrounding you.

Long before you called on the name of Jesus, the Lord was feeding you, preserving you, restraining evil, giving you breath, and causing the sun to rise on your days of rebellion. Long before you understood the gospel, you were living inside a world upheld by mercy—walking on earth that did not swallow you, breathing air you did not create, drinking water you did not form, and receiving moments of kindness you did not deserve.

This is a dimension of grace that many overlook: the grace of God that sustains His creation. It is the kindness of the Creator poured out over the whole earth—over the righteous and the unrighteous—so that no man can say, "God has not been good to me."

Jesus Himself proclaimed this in a way that should humble every heart:

"...for He makes His sun rise on the evil and on the good and sends rain on the just and on the unjust." (Matthew 5:45, NKJV)

The Lord does not only show goodness to those who worship Him. He shows goodness to those who ignore Him. He does not only send rain upon the praying home, but upon the blaspheming home. He does not only keep the believer alive, but keeps the unbeliever alive. This is not because sin is small—but because God is patient. This is not because judgment is gone—but because mercy is still speaking.

And this grace has a purpose: it is meant to lead to repentance.

1) The Grace of Breath: Life Itself Is Borrowed Mercy

Every breath is a gift. The believer does not "own" life—he receives it. The unbeliever does not "control" life—he borrows it. That you are alive at this very moment is proof that God has not yet closed the day of mercy.

The apostle Paul declared to the philosophers of Athens that God is the One:

"...who gives to all life, breath, and all things." (Acts 17:25, NKJV)

This is grace at the most basic level—existence itself. If God withdrew His hand, humanity would vanish in an instant. The heartbeat continues because God permits it. The lungs fill because God sustains them. The mind thinks because God maintains the order of creation.

The fact that man uses God's gifts to sin against God is one of the greatest evidences of human depravity—and one of the greatest evidences of God's longsuffering.

2) The Grace of Provision: God Feeds Even Those Who Forget Him

When Paul preached to the Gentiles in Lystra, he spoke of a God who had been kind to them even though they did not know His name:

"Nevertheless, He did not leave Himself without witness, in that He did good, gave us rain from heaven and fruitful seasons, filling our hearts with food and gladness." (Acts 14:17, NKJV)

Notice the phrase: "He did not leave Himself without witness." Creation is not silent. Providence is not accidental. Every harvest, every season, every provision, every table with food upon it is a testimony that God is good—even when men are not.

This is a fear-provoking truth: God was good to us while we were still sinners. Many people have enjoyed the gifts of God while mocking the Giver. Many have laughed in the sunshine while rejecting the Son. Many have eaten bread daily while refusing the Bread of Life.

And yet, God continues to witness to the human heart through His kindness.

3) The Grace of Restraint: God Holds Back What We Deserve

If God gave humanity the full harvest of his sin instantly, the earth would collapse under judgment. Yet God restrains. He delays. He holds back. He gives space. He gives time.

This restraint is not weakness. It is mercy.

"The Lord is not slack concerning His promise… but is longsuffering toward us, not willing that any should perish but that all should come to repentance." (2 Peter 3:9, NKJV)

The delay of judgment is a form of grace. The patience of God is a form of grace. The fact that the earth continues, societies continue, families continue—despite humanity's rebellion—is evidence that God is still extending mercy and calling men to turn.

But do not mistake restraint for approval. The fact that God has not judged yet does not mean God will not judge. It means God is giving time for repentance. That is why Scripture warns against interpreting patience as permission:

"Or do you despise the riches of His goodness, forbearance, and longsuffering, not knowing that the goodness of God leads you to repentance?" (Romans 2:4, NKJV)

To despise His goodness is not merely to insult it with words, but to abuse it with continued rebellion—to keep sinning while using God's kindness as a hiding place.

4) Common Grace Is Real—But It Is Not Salvation

Here we must be clear: the grace that sustains creation is different from the grace that saves. God can be good to a man without that man being born again. God can provide for a man while that man remains lost. God can protect a man from danger while that man still rejects Christ.

Common grace is God's kindness to all, but saving grace is God's redemption in Christ.

This is why it is possible for a person to experience many blessings and still perish—because blessings are not salvation, and provision is not reconciliation. Many have interpreted the gifts of God as proof that their soul is safe, but Scripture reveals that God's gifts are meant to awaken the heart to the Giver, not to lull the conscience into false peace.

Common grace is God's witness. It is the knocking on the door.

Saving grace is God's entrance. It is the new birth.

And the greatest tragedy is when a person enjoys the witness but rejects the Savior.

5) The Severity Hidden in Kindness: The Day of Mercy Has an End

Grace sustains the world, but it does not remove accountability. Mercy delays judgment, but it does not erase it. The same Bible that shows God feeding nations also shows God measuring nations. The same Bible that reveals God's patience also reveals God's wrath against unrepentant sin.

So common grace should not make anyone casual. It should make everyone tremble.

Every sunrise is God saying, "You have another chance."

Every breath is God saying, "Return to Me."

Every meal is God saying, "I am still kind."

Every moment of life is time borrowed from judgment.

And when you see it that way, you can no longer live carelessly. You begin to feel the weight of grace. You begin to recognize that God's kindness is holy. It is extended not because man is worthy, but because God is merciful.

6) A Word to the Believer: If God Sustains the World, How Much More Will He Sustain You?

Believer, if God's grace sustains those who hate Him, how much more will He sustain you who belong to Him? If He feeds the unbeliever, will He not strengthen His own child? If He gives rain to the rebel, will He not give help to the repentant?

Yet here is the other side that provokes godly fear: If the world is judged for rejecting grace, how much more serious is it for a believer to trample grace?

The believer has not only received sunshine and rain—he has received the blood of the covenant. The believer has not only tasted provision—he has tasted redemption. The believer has not only experienced kindness—he has received the Holy Spirit.

So, if common grace leaves the unbeliever without excuse, saving grace leaves the believer without excuse for complacency.

This is why we must not treat grace lightly. We must not live as though mercy is infinite time. We must not drift while claiming faith. We must not call Christ "Lord" while refusing obedience. The fear of the Lord is the beginning of wisdom—and it is also the guardian of grace.

Closing Scriptures for Meditation (NKJV)

- *"...He makes His sun rise on the evil and on the good, and sends rain on the just and on the unjust." (Matthew 5:45)*

- *"Nevertheless He did not leave Himself without witness... gave us rain... fruitful seasons..." (Acts 14:17)*

- *"Or do you despise the riches of His goodness... not knowing that the goodness of God leads you to repentance?" (Romans 2:4)*

CHAPTER THREE:
THE GRACE OF GOD THAT BRINGS SALVATION — GRACE APPEARED, AND HIS NAME IS JESUS

There is a grace that sustains the world, and there is a grace that saves the soul.

Common grace keeps breath in the lungs and rain on the field. But saving grace does something far greater: it brings the dead sinner back to God. It does not merely improve a life—it resurrects a heart. It does not merely clean the outside—it makes a man new from the inside. It does not merely delay judgment—it removes condemnation by placing the believer into Christ.

And the Holy Spirit declares the turning point of all history in one breathtaking sentence:

"For the grace of God that brings salvation has appeared to all men."
(Titus 2:11, NKJV)

Grace appeared. Grace did not remain distant. Grace stepped into time. Grace entered human suffering. Grace took on flesh. Grace walked among sinners. Grace was touched, rejected, mocked, crucified, buried—and rose again. This is not poetry. This is the gospel. Grace is not an idea floating in the air; it is the living intervention of God in the Person of Jesus Christ.

If you want to know what grace looks like, look at Jesus.

1) Grace Is God Coming Toward the Undeserving

Grace begins with God, not with man.

Man did not climb up to God. Man did not bargain his way into heaven. Man did not earn his rescue with religious effort. Scripture strips human pride down to nothing so that Christ alone may be exalted.

"But God demonstrates His own love toward us, in that while we were still sinners, Christ died for us." (Romans 5:8, NKJV)

Grace is the holy love of God moving toward those who have no claim on Him. Grace is mercy stepping into rebellion. Grace is God's rescue mission launched into a world that did not ask Him to come.

And this is why grace humbles the soul: because it destroys the lie that we deserved anything but judgment.

2) Saving Grace Has a Name: Jesus Christ Alone

In Titus 2:11, grace is not merely "given." Grace "appeared." That word points to a manifestation, an unveiling, a visible arrival. Grace took form. Grace came with a face. Grace came with a cross.

"For you know the grace of our Lord Jesus Christ, that though He was rich, yet for your sakes He became poor, that you through His poverty

might become rich." (2 Corinthians 8:9, NKJV)

The grace that saves is not generic kindness—it is Christ's incarnation, obedience, suffering, death, and resurrection. Grace is the Son of God stepping into our curse so that we could step into His blessing.

And Scripture refuses to share that glory with any other name.

"Nor is there salvation in any other, for there is no other name under heaven given among men by which we must be saved." (Acts 4:12, NKJV)

This is why this book must be clear from the beginning: saving grace is through Christ Jesus alone. Not Christ plus works. Not Christ plus religious rituals. Not Christ plus moral improvement. Not Christ plus human merit.

Christ alone.

3) Saving Grace Is Not "God Ignoring Sin"—It Is God Judging Sin in Christ

Many people think grace means God simply "lets things go." But the cross proves the opposite. Grace did not come because sin was small. Grace came because sin was deadly, and justice demanded payment.

At Calvary, God did not pretend sin was harmless. He crushed it. He judged it. He condemned it—in the body of His Son.

"For He made Him who knew no sin to be sin for us, that we might become the righteousness of God in Him." (2 Corinthians 5:21, NKJV)

This is the holiness inside grace. Grace is not God compromising with darkness. Grace is God defeating darkness at the cost of blood.

And that is why true grace produces godly fear. If sin required the death of the spotless Son of God, then sin must never be treated casually by those who claim His name.

4) Grace That Brings Salvation Is for All—But Not Automatically in All

Titus 2:11 says grace has appeared "to all men." That does not mean all men are saved automatically. It means the message has been revealed openly; the door has been unlocked; the invitation has gone out beyond Israel to the nations; the gospel is not hidden for a few—it is proclaimed to the world.

But salvation must be received.

"He came to His own, and His own did not receive Him. But as many as received Him, to them He gave the right to become children of God..." *(John 1:11–12, NKJV)*

Grace is offered to all. Christ is proclaimed to all. But only those who repent and believe receive what grace brings—salvation, reconciliation, adoption, and the gift of eternal life.

And when saving grace is resisted, the very grace that could have saved becomes a witness against the soul—because light rejected increases accountability.

5) "Not by Works"—Because Grace and Merit Cannot Mix

This is where human pride resists the gospel. The flesh wants to contribute. The religious spirit wants credit. But the Lord has designed salvation so that no man can boast and no flesh can glory.

"For by grace you have been saved through faith, and that not of yourselves; it is the gift of God, not of works, lest anyone should boast." *(Ephesians 2:8–9, NKJV)*

Grace is a gift. You do not earn a gift; you receive it. You do not negotiate a gift; you accept it. You do not deserve a gift; it is given freely.

And Paul seals this truth with a hammer:

"And if by grace, then it is no longer of works; otherwise grace is no longer grace." (Romans 11:6, NKJV)

Either salvation is grace, or it is wages. Either it is a gift, or it is a paycheck. Scripture refuses the mixture. Grace and self-righteousness cannot live in the same house.

6) Saved by Grace—For a Purpose: A Holy People

Here is where many stumble. They receive the truth that salvation is "not by works," and then they wrongly conclude that salvation produces no works. But the same passage that denies works as the cause of salvation immediately declares works as the fruit of salvation:

"For we are His workmanship, created in Christ Jesus for good works…" (Ephesians 2:10, NKJV)

Grace is not the enemy of holiness—grace is the foundation of holiness. Grace does not remove obedience; grace empowers obedience. Grace does not cancel righteousness; grace produces righteousness.

Titus will not allow any other interpretation:

"…teaching us that, denying ungodliness and worldly lusts, we should live soberly, righteously, and godly in the present age." (Titus 2:12, NKJV)

Grace that saves also teaches. Grace that rescues also trains. Grace that justifies also sanctifies.

So, if a man claims grace but lives in willful sin without repentance, he is not magnifying grace—he is mocking it. And if a man uses grace to excuse bondage, he has not understood grace at all.

7) A Call to Godly Fear: Do Not Resist the Grace That Appeared

Beloved, saving grace is the most precious treasure heaven has ever released into the earth. It is Christ offered freely to the guilty. It is pardon for rebels. It is cleansing for defiled hearts. It is adoption for the orphaned soul. It is reconciliation for the enemy of God.

And because it is so precious, Scripture calls us to respond with trembling gratitude—not with casual familiarity.

If grace appeared, then a decision is demanded.

- Will you receive Christ or reject Him?

- Will you repent or remain hardened?

- Will you bow to the Son or cling to self?

- Will you treat the blood as holy—or as common?

This is not a small matter. Eternity is in view.

"For the grace of God that brings salvation has appeared to all men."
(Titus 2:11, NKJV)

Grace has appeared. And the only safe response is humble surrender.

Closing Scriptures for Meditation (NKJV)

- *"For the grace of God that brings salvation has appeared to all men." (Titus 2:11)*

- *"For by grace you have been saved through faith... not of works..." (Ephesians 2:8–9)*

- *"And if by grace, then it is no longer of works..." (Romans 11:6)*

- *"But as many as received Him... to them He gave the right to become children of God..." (John 1:12)*

CHAPTER FOUR: GRACE THROUGH FAITH IN JESUS CHRIST ALONE — THE OPEN HAND THAT RECEIVES, THE HEART THAT SURRENDERS

Grace is God's gift. Faith is the hand that receives it.

Grace is the fountain. Faith is the cup.

Grace is the door opened by God. Faith is the step that enters.

This is why Scripture joins these two together with divine precision:

"For by grace you have been saved through faith..." (Ephesians 2:8, NKJV)

Grace is not earned. Faith is not payment. Faith is not a work that buys salvation. Faith is the humble response of a heart that believes God is true, believes Christ is sufficient, and comes to Him empty—depending on Him alone.

Yet here is where many are deceived: they speak of faith, but they do not obey Christ. They claim faith, but they will not repent. They confess Jesus with their mouth, but they deny Him with their lives. And because of this, the church must recover the biblical meaning of faith—not as mental agreement, but as surrendering trust.

Faith that receives grace is not shallow. It is not casual. It is not merely emotional. It is living.

1) Faith Is Trust in a Person, Not a Theory

Biblical faith is not faith in faith. It is not confidence in positive thinking. It is not religious optimism. Saving faith has an object: Jesus Christ Himself.

"But as many as received Him, to them He gave the right to become children of God, to those who believe in His name." (John 1:12, NKJV)

To "believe in His name" is more than acknowledging His existence. Even demons acknowledge that. Saving faith entrusts the soul to Christ—His death, His resurrection, His lordship, His Word, His power to save to the uttermost.

This faith says, "If You do not save me, I cannot be saved."

This faith says, "I have no righteousness of my own."

This faith says, "You are my only hope."

That is why the proud struggle with saving faith—because saving faith begins where self-confidence dies.

2) Faith Is Not a Work—But Faith Is Never Alone

The enemy has used a subtle twist to destroy many: he convinces people that since we are not saved by works, obedience does not matter. But Scripture does not teach that. Scripture teaches:

- We are not saved by works, so no man can boast.

- But we are saved unto good works, because grace changes the life.

"For we are His workmanship, created in Christ Jesus for good works…" (Ephesians 2:10, NKJV)

Works are not the root of salvation; they are the fruit. Obedience does not purchase grace; it proves grace has truly been received. Holiness does not earn adoption; it reveals the reality of sonship.

So, the question is not, "Do you have a religious confession?"

The question is, "Has faith united you to Christ so that your life is being transformed?"

3) True Faith Produces Repentance Because It Sees God Clearly

Faith is not just believing that Jesus can forgive. Faith is believing that Jesus is Lord—and therefore sin must be forsaken.

Repentance is not a "work" that competes with grace. Repentance is the turning of the heart that happens when grace is genuinely believed. When a man sees God's holiness and God's kindness together, the soul cannot remain casual.

"Or do you despise the riches of His goodness… not knowing that the goodness of God leads you to repentance?" (Romans 2:4, NKJV)

Grace leads. Faith follows. And the path faith follows is repentance—turning from darkness to light, from self-rule to Christ's rule, from sin as a secret lover to Christ as supreme treasure.

A faith that refuses repentance is not saving faith—it is a dead claim.

4) Faith Receives Justification, Not Self-Righteousness

Justification is one of the most humbling gifts in Scripture: God declares the guilty righteous—not because they became righteous by works, but because they were united to Christ by faith.

"...being justified freely by His grace through the redemption that is in Christ Jesus." (Romans 3:24, NKJV)

You are not justified because you improved. You are justified because Christ paid. You are not justified because you became worthy. You are justified because He is worthy.

And this is where godly fear must be restored: if God justifies by grace through faith, then a believer must never treat sin lightly, as though justification is a small thing. The one who has been declared righteous has been bought with blood. The one justified is now called to live as one who belongs to Another.

5) Faith Continues: Grace Is Entered by Faith and We Stand by Faith

Many believers understand faith only as a doorway. But Scripture speaks of faith as a walk—a continuing reliance on Christ.

"...we have access by faith into this grace in which we stand..."
(Romans 5:2, NKJV)

We do not only enter grace by faith—we stand in grace by faith. We do not only begin in the Spirit—we must continue in the Spirit. We do not only start by trusting Christ—we must keep trusting Him, especially under pressure, temptation, and suffering.

This destroys the lie of a casual gospel that says, "It doesn't matter how you live; you prayed a prayer once."

No—Scripture calls believers to abide, continue, endure, and hold fast.

Faith is not a momentary decision; it is a living bond with Christ.

6) Faith That Saves Is Faith That Abides in Christ

Jesus did not describe salvation as a one-time emotion. He described it as abiding union:

"Abide in Me, and I in you... He who abides in Me, and I in him, bears much fruit..." (John 15:4–5, NKJV)

This is where grace and faith become living reality: grace supplies; faith abides. Grace empowers; faith depends. Grace strengthens; faith clings to Christ and refuses to let go.

And if a man claims faith but bears no fruit—no hatred of sin, no love for holiness, no pursuit of God, no obedience to Christ—he is not honoring grace. He is resisting the very grace he claims.

"Thus also faith by itself, if it does not have works, is dead." (James 2:17, NKJV)

James is not contradicting grace. James is protecting grace from counterfeit faith. He is saying that true faith lives, moves, and obeys, because Christ lives within the believer.

7) A Warning That Restores Godly Fear: Do Not Trade Living Faith for Religious Confidence

Here is the danger that has destroyed many: religious confidence without living faith.

People learn Christian language. They learn to say "grace." They learn to say "I'm saved." They learn to say "I believe." But their hearts do not tremble at sin. Their eyes do not weep over compromise. Their lives do not bow to Christ's Word.

This is a deadly place—not because grace is weak, but because the heart can become deceived.

The grace of God is not a license.

Faith is not an excuse.

Salvation is not a costume.

Christ is not a slogan.

Grace through faith means the believer becomes Christ's possession—His bondservant, His disciple, His temple.

Therefore, let every believer hear this in godly fear: if we say we have faith, let us prove it by abiding, obeying, repenting quickly, and walking in the light—because grace is too holy to be used as a hiding place for darkness.

Closing Scriptures for Meditation (NKJV)

- *"For by grace you have been saved through faith…" (Ephesians 2:8)*

- *"…we have access by faith into this grace in which we stand…" (Romans 5:2)*

- *"Abide in Me… he who abides… bears much fruit." (John 15:4–5)*

- *"Faith by itself, if it does not have works, is dead." (James 2:17)*

CHAPTER FIVE:
SAVED BY GRACE — NOT BY WORKS, BUT BY THE WASHING OF REGENERATION AND RENEWAL OF THE HOLY SPIRIT

If there is any truth that destroys human pride at the root, it is this: salvation is not earned. It is not purchased by religious effort, moral performance, church attendance, sacraments, family lineage, or personal discipline. If salvation could be earned, heaven would be filled with boasting. If salvation could be achieved by works, the cross would be unnecessary.

But God has written salvation in such a way that no flesh can glory—so that Christ alone is magnified.

The apostle Paul speaks with absolute clarity:

"Not by works of righteousness which we have done, but according to His mercy He saved us, through the washing of regeneration and renewing of the Holy Spirit." (Titus 3:5, NKJV)

This verse is not merely a statement—it is a holy rebuke to every form of self-righteousness. It is God shutting the mouth of human pride. It is the Lord saying, "You cannot save yourself. You cannot cleanse yourself. You cannot birth yourself into My Kingdom. You must be saved by My mercy."

And yet, this same verse is also comfort for the broken. Because if salvation is not by works of righteousness, then the sinner who has nothing to offer—no résumé, no religious record, no moral perfection—can still be saved. The door is open to the needy. The gospel is good news to the helpless.

1) "Not by Works of Righteousness" — The Death of Self-Salvation

Many people misunderstand why works cannot save. It is not because works are always evil. It is because works cannot remove guilt. Works cannot erase sin. Works cannot change the nature of the heart. Works can polish the outside while the inside remains dead.

A man can reform habits and still be unregenerate.

A man can join a church and still be unchanged.

A man can become religious and still be far from God.

The Lord does not merely want behavior modification—He requires new birth.

This is why grace must be preached with godly fear: salvation is not "God helping you become better." Salvation is "God raising you from death to life." Salvation is not rehabilitation; it is resurrection.

2) Salvation Is Mercy Flowing Through Grace

Paul says, "according to His mercy He saved us." Mercy is God withholding what we deserve. Grace is God giving what we do not deserve. Mercy removes the sentence. Grace gives new life. Mercy cancels judgment. Grace grants righteousness, adoption, and the Spirit.

This is why salvation is never casual. It is holy mercy.

When you understand mercy, you cannot treat grace like a common thing. If you truly see what you deserved—wrath, separation, eternal judgment—then grace becomes precious beyond words. You stop speaking of salvation as a small religious decision. You begin to tremble with gratitude because you realize: you were rescued from a real hell by a real Savior through a real cross.

3) "Washing of Regeneration" — Grace Does Not Only Forgive; It Cleanses and Recreates

Titus 3:5 does not stop at "He saved us." It tells us how He saved us: "through the washing of regeneration."

Regeneration means new birth—new life implanted by God. It is not merely cleaning the old; it is creating the new. It is not merely covering sin; it is changing the sinner. It is the miracle Jesus spoke of to Nicodemus:

"Most assuredly, I say to you, unless one is born again, he cannot see the kingdom of God." (John 3:3, NKJV)

Many want forgiveness without transformation. But biblical salvation includes both. The blood of Jesus cleanses the conscience, and the Spirit of God births a new nature. Grace does not leave you as you were; grace makes you a new creation.

"Therefore, if anyone is in Christ, he is a new creation; old things have passed away; behold, all things have become new." (2 Corinthians 5:17, NKJV)

This is why a gospel that tells people they are saved while remaining slaves to willful sin is a false comfort. Grace saves. Grace regenerates. Grace produces new life. And that new life begins to hate what it once loved and love what it once hated.

4) "Renewing of the Holy Spirit" — Saving Grace Brings the Spirit's Ongoing Work

Salvation is not only a moment—it is the beginning of a life under the Spirit's renewing power.

"...and renewing of the Holy Spirit." (Titus 3:5, NKJV)

The Holy Spirit renews the mind, convicts the heart, strengthens the inner man, and forms Christ within the believer. Grace does not leave a believer to fight alone; it gives the Spirit as Helper, Teacher, Comforter, and Sanctifier.

Here is where godly fear must remain: if saving grace includes the Holy Spirit's renewing, then resisting the Spirit is not a light thing. Quenching conviction is not a small matter. Ignoring the Spirit's warning is how believers drift into darkness while still speaking Christian language.

Grace brings the Spirit. And the Spirit calls you into holiness.

5) Titus 3:7 — Justified by Grace, Made Heirs by Hope

Paul continues:

"...that having been justified by His grace we should become heirs according to the hope of eternal life." (Titus 3:7, NKJV)

Justification means God declares the believing sinner righteous—based on Christ's righteousness, not his own. This is the divine verdict over the believer: "Not guilty." "Accepted." "Righteous in My Son."

But notice what follows: "heirs... hope of eternal life." Grace does not merely save you from something; it saves you unto something. It makes you an heir of God, a citizen of heaven, a son or daughter with a living hope.

Yet here also is the holy warning: heirs must live as heirs. Children must walk as children. Those who have been justified by grace must not return to the mud with casual hearts.

When grace is real, it creates reverence. It creates gratitude. It creates a new hunger to please God—not to earn salvation, but because the heart has been made alive.

6) A Deep Call to Godly Fear: Do Not Reduce Salvation to Words

Beloved, salvation is not a slogan. It is not "I said a prayer." It is not "I grew up in church." It is not "I believe God exists."

Salvation is regeneration.

Salvation is renewal by the Spirit.

Salvation is justification by grace.

Salvation is a new life that begins to bear fruit.

So, hear the seriousness: if the Holy Spirit has truly regenerated a man, that man cannot comfortably live in willful sin without repentance. He may stumble, but he cannot settle. He may fall, but he cannot make peace with darkness. Something inside him fights back   because grace is alive within him.

This is not legalism. This is life.

The most dangerous form of deception is not outright atheism—it is Christian words without Christian life. It is claiming grace while despising the One who gives it. It is speaking of salvation while rejecting repentance. It is being content with a form of godliness while denying its power.

Saving grace is power. Saving grace is new birth. Saving grace is the Holy Spirit's work. And saving grace must never be taken for granted.

Closing Scriptures for Meditation (NKJV)

- *"Not by works of righteousness which we have done, but according to His mercy He saved us..." (Titus 3:5)*

- *"...through the washing of regeneration and renewing of the Holy Spirit." (Titus 3:5)*

- *"...justified by His grace... heirs according to the hope of eternal life." (Titus 3:7)*

- *"Unless one is born again, he cannot see the kingdom of God." (John 3:3)*

CHAPTER SIX:
"My Grace Is Sufficient" — Sustaining Grace in Weakness, Trials, Temptation, and Spiritual Warfare

There is a grace that saves you in a moment—

and there is a grace that keeps you in the long war.

Many believers love the message of saving grace, but they do not yet understand sustaining grace. They rejoice that Christ forgave them, yet they stumble when affliction continues. They celebrate the cross, yet they fear when weakness remains. They pray, they fast, they cry out—yet the thorn does not leave, the pressure does not lift, the temptation still knocks, and the battle still rages.

And it is there—right where human strength ends—that the Lord speaks one of the most life-altering words a believer can ever hear:

"And He said to me, 'My grace is sufficient for you, for My strength is made perfect in weakness.' Therefore most gladly I will rather boast in my infirmities, that the power of Christ may rest upon me." (2 Corinthians 12:9, NKJV)

This is not a poetic statement. This is a spiritual law. The Lord does not always remove the weight—but He supplies strength under it. He does not always take away the battle—but He gives grace to stand in it. He does not always silence the storm—but He gives power to endure, and faith to obey, and holiness to overcome.

And here is where godly fear must be restored: if God gives sufficient grace, then no believer can use weakness as an excuse for willful sin. Grace does not erase responsibility; it empowers obedience. The grace that sustains is not permission to surrender—it is power to endure.

1) Paul's Thorn and Heaven's Answer: Grace, Not Escape

Paul pleaded three times that the thorn might depart. He was not casual. He was not lazy. He was not content with pain. He prayed earnestly.

Yet God's answer was not removal. God's answer was grace.

This reveals something that cuts against modern Christianity: we often seek deliverance from discomfort more than we seek transformation into Christlikeness. But God is more committed to your holiness than your convenience. He is more committed to your eternal maturity than your temporary ease.

Sometimes the Lord allows what breaks human pride so that the believer learns divine dependence. And dependence is not weakness—it is wisdom.

"Therefore most gladly I will rather boast in my infirmities, that the

power of Christ may rest upon me." (2 Corinthians 12:9, NKJV)

Grace was not only forgiveness for Paul—it was power resting upon him.

2) "Sufficient" Means Enough—Enough to Endure, Enough to Obey, Enough to Overcome

The word "sufficient" does not mean "barely surviving." It means enough. Enough supply for the demand. Enough strength for the assignment. Enough help for the need.

When God says, "My grace is sufficient," He is declaring:

- Enough grace for your temptation

- Enough grace for your grief

- Enough grace for your pressure

- Enough grace for your weakness

- Enough grace for your warfare

- Enough grace for your calling

- Enough grace to keep you from falling into darkness if you will abide in Him

This is why sustaining grace should produce confidence—not in self, but in God. The believer who truly trusts sustaining grace stops glorifying his weakness and starts glorifying Christ's strength.

3) Sustaining Grace Is How God Keeps the Believer from Drifting

Many believers do not fall into ruin suddenly. They drift. They become tired. They become prayerless. They become careless. They start tolerating what they once resisted. They start excusing what they once confessed.

But sustaining grace works like a holy anchor. It strengthens the inner man. It stirs conviction. It renews desire. It calls the believer back to the secret place. It revives hunger for the Word. It empowers repentance. It rebuilds spiritual discipline—not as dead religion, but as living communion.

This is why the writer of Hebrews warns:

"Looking carefully lest anyone fall short of the grace of God..."
(Hebrews 12:15, NKJV)

How can someone "fall short" of grace? Not because grace runs out—but because the heart stops drawing near. The believer begins to live as though grace is automatic while neglecting prayer, neglecting the Word, neglecting repentance, and neglecting the fear of God.

Sustaining grace is received as we abide, seek, humble ourselves, and come boldly to the throne. Not to earn grace—but to receive the grace that God freely gives.

4) Grace in Temptation: God Gives Power to Say "No"

Here is a crucial truth for godly fear: the grace of God does not merely forgive sin after it happens—it gives power to resist sin before it happens.

Paul teaches that grace trains us:

"For the grace of God that brings salvation has appeared to all men,
teaching us that, denying ungodliness and worldly lusts, we should
live soberly, righteously, and godly in the present age." (Titus 2:11–12,
NKJV)

Grace teaches denial. Grace trains refusal. Grace strengthens self-control. Grace does not whisper, "It doesn't matter." Grace thunders quietly in the conscience: "You belong to Christ. Come out from that."

And when temptation rises, Scripture does not say the believer is helpless:

"No temptation has overtaken you except such as is common to man; but God is faithful... will also make the way of escape..." (1 Corinthians 10:13, NKJV)

The "way of escape" is often not a change in circumstance—it is grace given in the moment to obey. Sometimes the escape is to run. Sometimes it is to shut the door. Sometimes it is to confess. Sometimes it is to endure and not give in. But God is faithful to provide sufficient grace.

So, a believer cannot honestly say, "I had no choice." If you are in Christ, and you are walking in the Spirit, grace gives power to resist. If you fall, you repent quickly—but you do not make peace with bondage.

5) Grace in Spiritual Warfare: Power to Stand

Many believers think warfare is fought only with loud prayers. But warfare is fought most deeply in holiness, obedience, and endurance—because sin gives the enemy legal footholds, but grace empowers the believer to close those doors.

Sustaining grace strengthens the believer to stand in the armor of God, to resist the devil, and to remain steadfast. The Christian life is not a playground—it is a battlefield. And grace is heaven's supply line to keep the believer from collapsing in the fight.

And here is the sobering truth: some fall not because the devil is too strong, but because they treated grace too lightly—neglecting prayer, embracing secret sin, feeding the flesh, and silencing conviction. The enemy does not need to overpower the believer if he can seduce the believer into carelessness.

Sustaining grace restores sobriety. It restores alertness. It produces godly fear. It teaches the believer to watch and pray.

6) "Strength Made Perfect in Weakness" — The Mystery of Grace

God's strength is not "made perfect" because weakness is good in itself. It is made perfect because weakness forces dependence.

When a believer recognizes, "I cannot do this without You," the door opens for Christ's power to rest upon him. But when a believer becomes self-confident—prayerless, careless, independent—he becomes spiritually vulnerable even if he looks strong outwardly.

This is why grace often leads us into humble places. It kills pride. It breaks self-reliance. It teaches us to walk softly before God.

And this is also why grace must never be taken for granted: the moment a believer treats grace as a guarantee while living in compromise is the moment he begins to drift toward spiritual disaster.

7) A Call to Godly Fear: Do Not Use "Weakness" to Justify Disobedience

Beloved, weakness is real. Trials are real. Pain is real. But grace is also real—and it is sufficient.

So, we must say this with trembling and love:

Do not call disobedience "weakness."

Do not call rebellion "struggle."

Do not call bondage "personality."

Do not call compromise "grace."

When the Lord says, "My grace is sufficient," He is not giving us a license to remain in darkness—He is giving us power to come out.

If you have fallen, run to the throne of grace.

If you are weary, draw near again.

If you are tempted, ask for help now.

If you are wounded, seek healing.

If you are drifting, repent quickly.

The grace of God is not only a safety net—it is a holy power meant to keep you walking with Christ until the end.

Closing Scriptures for Meditation (NKJV)

- *"My grace is sufficient for you, for My strength is made perfect in weakness." (2 Corinthians 12:9)*

- *"Looking carefully lest anyone fall short of the grace of God..." (Hebrews 12:15)*

- *"The grace of God... teaching us... denying ungodliness..." (Titus 2:11–12)*

- *"God is faithful... will make the way of escape..." (1 Corinthians 10:13)*

Chapter Seven: Justified by Grace — Declared Righteous, Called to Walk Worthy, and Warned Not to Turn Grace into a Cover for Sin

There is a grace that rescues the guilty, and there is a grace that declares the guilty righteous.

This is one of the most staggering realities in the whole counsel of God: that the Judge of all the earth can look at a sinner who deserves judgment and declare, "Righteous." Not because the sinner earned it, not because the sinner achieved moral perfection, not because the sinner proved himself— but because that sinner has been united to Jesus Christ by faith. Christ took the condemnation. Christ provided the righteousness.

Christ bore the wrath. And grace delivers the verdict.

Paul speaks plainly:

"...that having been justified by His grace we should become heirs according to the hope of eternal life." (Titus 3:7, NKJV)

Justification is not a feeling. It is not an emotional moment. It is a legal, divine declaration—God's courtroom verdict over the believer: not guilty. Accepted. Cleansed. Counted righteous in Christ.

And because it is so glorious, it must also be protected—because many have used this truth not to honor God, but to excuse sin. This chapter is written to restore both comfort and fear: comfort for the repentant, and fear for the careless.

1) What Does "Justified" Mean?

To be justified is to be declared righteous. It is God's act of acquitting the guilty sinner and counting him righteous because of Christ.

"Therefore, having been justified by faith, we have peace with God through our Lord Jesus Christ." (Romans 5:1, NKJV)

Notice: justified by faith—because faith joins us to Christ, the Righteous One. Justification is not God pretending you are righteous while you remain unchanged; it is God declaring you righteous because Christ's righteousness is credited to you, and His blood has cleansed you.

Justification answers the most terrifying question the human soul can face:

How can I be right with a holy God?

And the gospel answers: by grace.

2) Justified Freely — Grace Removes Boasting

Paul leaves no room for pride:

"...being justified freely by His grace through the redemption that is in Christ Jesus." (Romans 3:24, NKJV)

"Freely" means without cost to the receiver—yet not without cost to the Redeemer. Grace is free to you because Christ paid the price.

This kills all boasting. No man stands in heaven and says, "I earned my place." Heaven will be filled with one song: Worthy is the Lamb.

So, if you have been justified by grace, you cannot remain proud. True justification produces humility. It produces gratitude. It produces a trembling love. It makes you hate sin—not only because sin is wrong, but because sin cost your Savior His blood.

3) Justification Brings Peace — But Not Peace with Sin

Justification brings peace with God.

"We have peace with God..." (Romans 5:1, NKJV)

But here is where deception enters: many confuse peace with God with peace with sin. They assume that since they are justified, sin is no longer serious. They treat grace like an insurance policy instead of a holy covenant.

But Scripture never uses justification to make believers careless. Scripture uses justification to make believers secure in God and severe against sin.

God gives peace with Himself so the believer can walk in holiness— not so the believer can return to darkness without fear.

4) Justification Is a Door into a New Realm: "This Grace in Which We Stand"

Paul continues:

"Through whom also we have access by faith into this grace in which we stand..." (Romans 5:2, NKJV)

Justification is not only a verdict; it is an entrance into a new standing. The believer is no longer standing in Adam, under condemnation. He is standing in Christ, under grace.

But standing in grace is not passive. It is a holy position that demands a holy response. When you stand in grace, you stand in a realm where Christ is Lord, the Spirit is active, the Word is living, and sin is no longer your master.

5) A Necessary Question: If I Am Justified by Grace, Can I Live in Willful Sin?

This question has become a battlefield in modern Christianity. Many use grace to silence conviction. Many quote justification to cancel the fear of God. Many speak of the cross while remaining enslaved to secret darkness.

So, we must answer with Scripture, not opinions.

Paul expected this exact abuse and responded with thunder:

"What shall we say then? Shall we continue in sin that grace may abound? Certainly not! How shall we who died to sin live any longer in it?" (Romans 6:1–2, NKJV)

Grace does not give permission to continue in sin. Grace delivers from sin's dominion. If a man claims to be justified but refuses repentance, refuses holiness, refuses submission to Christ—he is not honoring grace. He is proving he has not truly died to sin.

A justified believer may stumble, yes—but he cannot make peace with sin. He cannot live comfortably in darkness. He cannot sin boldly while claiming grace without fear. If he can, something is wrong in the heart.

6) The Warning of Hebrews: Grace Can Be Treated with Contempt

Hebrews speaks with a seriousness that should shake every careless soul:

"...how much worse punishment, do you suppose, will he be thought worthy who has trampled the Son of God underfoot, counted the blood of the covenant by which he was sanctified a common thing, and insulted the Spirit of grace?" (Hebrews 10:29, NKJV)

That phrase— "Spirit of grace"—is terrifying and beautiful. Grace is not only a doctrine; it is the Spirit's holy work. To "insult" the Spirit of grace is to treat the blood as common, to treat conviction as annoying, to treat repentance as optional, and to treat sin as safe.

This is why godly fear must return: you cannot play with grace.

7) Justification Must Lead to Sanctification — Grace That Declares Also Trains

The same letter that proclaims justification by grace also proclaims that grace trains us to live godly.

"For the grace of God... teaching us that, denying ungodliness... we should live soberly, righteously, and godly..." (Titus 2:11–12, NKJV)

Justification is the root; sanctification is the fruit.

Justification changes your standing; sanctification changes your walk.

Justification declares you righteous in Christ; sanctification forms Christ in you.

If justification does not produce sanctification, then the person is holding a doctrine without possessing the life.

8) A Word to the Tender Conscience: Justification Is Your Refuge

This chapter is not written to crush the repentant believer. It is written to awaken the careless one.

If you have stumbled and your heart is broken—run to Christ. Justification by grace is the refuge for the contrite. God is not calling you to hide; He is calling you to return. The blood of Jesus is sufficient. The throne of grace is open. Confess, forsake, and come back quickly.

But if you are sinning willfully and excusing it with grace, hear this in godly fear: you are not safe. You are not honoring Christ. You are insulting the Spirit of grace. And unless you repent, the very doctrine you claim will rise as a witness against you.

Closing Scriptures for Meditation (NKJV)

- *"...justified by His grace..." (Titus 3:7)*

- *"...justified freely by His grace..." (Romans 3:24)*

- *"Shall we continue in sin that grace may abound? Certainly not!" (Romans 6:1–2)*

- *"...insulted the Spirit of grace..." (Hebrews 10:29)*

CHAPTER EIGHT: SHAPED BY GRACE — GRACE THAT TRAINS THE SOUL, BREAKS THE POWER OF SIN, AND FORMS CHRIST WITHIN

(Going Deeper: Grace as Holy Training, Not Religious Permission)

Many believers have been taught to think of grace as God's willingness to forgive. And that is true—gloriously true. But if we stop there, we will never understand why so many Christians remain bound, unstable, double-minded, and spiritually dry while still using the language of grace.

Because biblical grace is not only pardon. Biblical grace is power.

Grace does not only rescue you from judgment. It re-forms you into a new kind of person.

Grace does not only wipe the record clean. It begins to write Christ into your life.

And Scripture makes this unmistakable:

"For the grace of God that brings salvation has appeared to all men, teaching us that, denying ungodliness and worldly lusts, we should live soberly, righteously, and godly in the present age." (Titus 2:11–12, NKJV)

That word "teaching" is the doorway into deeper understanding. It does not mean grace merely informs the mind. It means grace trains the life. Grace becomes a holy instructor—like a father disciplining a son, like a master shaping a servant, like a potter forming clay. Grace doesn't just say, "You are forgiven." Grace says, "Now come—learn My ways."

If your "grace" has never taught you to deny sin, it is not the grace of Titus 2.

1) The Deeper Meaning of "Teaching" — Grace as Training and Discipline

In Titus 2:12, the idea is not a classroom lecture; it is training—discipline that shapes character over time. Grace does not treat sin lightly because grace knows what sin does to the soul. Grace knows sin hardens the conscience, darkens the mind, grieves the Spirit, and pulls the heart away from intimacy with God.

So, grace trains you the way a loving father trains a child—firmly, patiently, persistently.

Not to shame you.

Not to condemn you.

But to make you whole.

Grace is God's spiritual training system. And training always involves resistance, correction, and growth. This is why grace cannot be reduced to a comforting message only. Grace comforts—yes. But grace also confronts. Grace heals—yes. But grace also cuts away what is diseased.

Grace is gentle enough to restore the fallen, and strong enough to break the chains of the stubborn.

2) The Two Holy Movements of Grace: "Denying" and "Living"

Titus 2:12 reveals two movements that grace produces:

1.   Denying ungodliness and worldly lusts

2.   Living soberly, righteously, and godly

Grace is not only subtraction; it is also addition.

Grace removes what corrupts, and it builds what reflects Christ.

A) Denying Ungodliness

To deny ungodliness is to reject what God rejects. It is to refuse agreement with sin. It is to stop calling darkness "human weakness" when it is rebellion. It is to stop negotiating with what Christ died to destroy.

Grace teaches the believer to say, "No."

No to lust.

No to bitterness.

No to compromise.

No to secret filth.

No to pride.

No to unforgiveness.

No to idolatry.

Not with self-will alone—but with Spirit-empowered resolve.

B) Living Soberly, Righteously, Godly

Grace teaches the believer what to build in place of what was removed:

- Soberly: self-controlled, watchful, spiritually awake

- Righteously: upright, obedient, clean before God and man

- Godly: reverent, God-centered, pursuing holiness and intimacy

This is not legalism. This is grace training the redeemed.

3) Grace Is Not "Leniency"—Grace Is Holy Power That Costs Blood

We must go deeper here: grace is precious because grace is costly.

Many have turned grace into a sentimental word—light, soft, unthreatening. But the cross forbids that. If grace came through the death of the Son of God, then grace is the most serious gift the universe has ever seen.

When a believer lives casually in sin while claiming grace, he is not magnifying grace—he is treating the blood as common.

Hebrews warns with frightening clarity:

"...counted the blood of the covenant by which he was sanctified a common thing, and insulted the Spirit of grace?" (Hebrews 10:29, NKJV)

Grace is not casual because the cross was not casual.

Grace is not cheap because redemption was not cheap.

Grace is not permission because Calvary was not permission—it was judgment.

So, grace must produce godly fear: fear to offend the Holy Spirit, fear to trample the Son, fear to treat holy things as common.

4) Grace Shapes the Inner Man — It Targets Desire, Not Just Behavior

Here is why many remain stuck: they try to change behavior without allowing grace to reshape desire.

Grace works deeper than habits. Grace goes into motives, cravings, imaginations, and affections. Grace does not only restrain sin, its re-orders love. It teaches the soul to love what is holy and hate what is defiled.

This is why true grace produces a new grief over sin. The believer begins to feel sin differently. What once felt normal begins to feel heavy. What once felt pleasurable begins to feel poisonous. What once felt secret begins to feel shameful—not because of man, but because the Spirit is tenderizing the conscience.

Grace makes the heart sensitive again.

And sensitivity is a gift. A hardened heart is a dangerous heart. A numb conscience is a terrifying place. When grace shapes a believer, the conscience becomes alive, and conviction becomes sacred—not as condemnation, but as protection.

5) Grace Is the Holy Environment Where Christ Is Formed in You

Grace is not only a gift given to you; it is an environment created around you—so Christ can be formed within.

Paul spoke of this burden:

"My little children, for whom I labor in birth again until Christ is

formed in you." (Galatians 4:19, NKJV)

This is what grace is aiming at: not merely that you stop sinning, but that you begin resembling Christ. That your reactions change. That your speech changes. That your desires change. That your thought-life changes. That your appetite shifts from worldly lust to spiritual hunger.

Grace forms Christ in the believer by:

- teaching the Word with clarity

- convicting with precision

- empowering obedience

- strengthening endurance

- humbling pride

- deepening intimacy

- increasing hatred for sin

- growing love for holiness

This is why grace is unquenchable—but the believer must cooperate with it. Grace does not force; grace trains. Grace does not drag; grace leads. Grace does not override the will; grace persuades the heart through truth, fear of the Lord, and love.

6) A Deep Warning: "Receiving Grace" Is Not the Same as "Being Shaped by Grace"

It is possible to taste grace and still resist grace.

The gospel can touch the lips while never conquering the heart. A person can love the idea of forgiveness while hating the call to holiness. A person can celebrate mercy while despising correction.

But Titus 2 exposes counterfeit grace: saving grace teaches, and the taught life changes.

So let this holy question search the reader:

- Has grace trained me to deny ungodliness?

- Do I repent quickly when convicted?

- Is my conscience tender or numb?

- Do I hate what Christ died for?

- Do I hunger for the Word and prayer?

- Do I desire holiness, or do I secretly protect sin?

These are not questions meant to produce despair; they are questions meant to produce truth—because truth leads to repentance, and repentance leads to life.

7) How Grace Shapes You Practically (The Path of a Trained Life)

Grace shapes a believer through consistent holy patterns:

1. Word — letting Scripture correct, cleanse, and renew the mind

2. Prayer — living before God, not merely visiting Him

3. Repentance — quick turning, swift confession, forsaking sin

4. Fellowship — walking in the light, refusing isolation and secrecy

5. Discipline — cutting off what feeds the flesh; fasting, self-control

6. Obedience — doing what God says even when feelings resist

7. Fear of the Lord — guarding the heart from casualness

This is not salvation by works. This is the outworking of grace in a life that is truly saved.

8) Closing Exhortation: Let Grace Train You, Not Excuse You

Beloved, grace is unquenchable—but you must not treat it as harmless. Grace is tender—but it is also holy. Grace is merciful—but it is also severe toward sin. Grace saves—but it also shapes. Grace forgives—but it also forms.

Do not use grace to protect what God is trying to remove.

Do not call grace what the Bible calls lewdness.

Do not silence conviction and call it peace.

Do not ignore correction and call it freedom.

Instead, yield. Let grace teach you. Let grace discipline you. Let grace reshape you until Christ is seen in you.

Because in the end, the true evidence that grace has appeared is not only that you say you are saved—but that you are being trained to live godly in the present age.

Closing Scriptures for Meditation (NKJV)

- *"For the grace of God... has appeared... teaching us that, denying ungodliness..." (Titus 2:11–12)*

- *"...counted the blood of the covenant... a common thing... insulted the Spirit of grace..." (Hebrews 10:29)*

- *"...until Christ is formed in you." (Galatians 4:19)*

CHAPTER NINE: FUELED BY GRACE — THE DIVINE SUPPLY THAT EMPOWERS OBEDIENCE, ENDURANCE, AND PERSEVERANCE TO THE END

Grace does not only save you. Grace does not only shape you.

Grace fuels you.

Many believers know grace as forgiveness, yet they try to live the Christian life by human strength. They begin in the Spirit and then try to finish in the flesh—striving, struggling, burning out, collapsing, repeating cycles, and wondering why their devotion fades. They love God, but they lack endurance. They want holiness, but they feel powerless. They desire consistency, but their spiritual life rises and falls like a wave.

This is where the Lord wants to reveal a deeper dimension: grace is not only God's favor toward you—it is God's power within you. Grace is heaven's supply line. Grace is spiritual fuel. Grace is strength given to the inner man so you can obey, endure, resist darkness, and remain faithful.

And Scripture speaks of grace in this living way:

"And God is able to make all grace abound toward you, that you, always having all sufficiency in all things, may have an abundance for every good work." (2 Corinthians 9:8, NKJV)

Grace abounds toward you so that you may abound in good works. That is fuel. That is supply. That is divine enabling.

1) Grace Is Not Only a Gift Given Once — It Is a Supply Given Continually

Many treat grace as a single moment: "I got saved by grace." True. But grace is also a continual strengthening: "I am kept by grace."

Peter speaks of God as the God of "all grace":

"But may the God of all grace, who called us to His eternal glory by Christ Jesus, after you have suffered a while, perfect, establish, strengthen, and settle you." (1 Peter 5:10, NKJV)

Notice what grace does: it perfects, establishes, strengthens, settles. That is not merely pardon. That is power to mature.

The believer is not meant to live on yesterday's grace. Grace is like manna—received daily, drawn continually, relied upon constantly. When believers grow prayerless, they do not lose God's love, but they cut themselves off from the experience of divine supply. They begin running on fumes.

2) Grace Fuels Obedience: The Strength to Do What God Commands

One of the greatest lies in the church is that obedience is legalism. No—obedience is love. And grace is what empowers it.

Jesus said:

"If you love Me, keep My commandments." (John 14:15, NKJV)

But how does a weak human being keep the commandments of a holy God? By grace. Grace does not lower God's standard; grace lifts the believer into God's standard. Grace does not excuse disobedience; grace empowers obedience.

Paul understood this mystery. He labored, yet he refused to take credit:

"But by the grace of God I am what I am... I labored more abundantly than they all, yet not I, but the grace of God which was with me." (1 Corinthians 15:10, NKJV)

Grace "with me." Grace present. Grace enabling. Grace powering holy labor.

So, when the believer says, "I cannot obey," the Spirit gently answers, "You cannot—without grace. But you can with grace."

3) Grace Fuels Repentance: Power to Turn Quickly and Fully

Some think repentance is only for the beginning of salvation. But repentance is also how believers stay clean, stay tender, and stay close to God.

Grace fuels repentance by:

- keeping the conscience alive

- strengthening humility to confess

- giving courage to forsake sin

- restoring the heart when it falls

- producing godly sorrow that leads to life

The more grace fuels you, the quicker you turn. The quicker you confess. The faster you flee darkness. The less you negotiate with sin.

This is one of the marks of a life fueled by grace: repentance becomes swift and compromise becomes intolerable.

4) Grace Fuels Endurance: Strength Under Pressure, Not Only Escape from It

Many believers think strength means the absence of weakness. But Scripture teaches something deeper: strength is God's power manifested through weakness.

"My grace is sufficient for you..." (2 Corinthians 12:9, NKJV)

When grace fuels endurance, the believer may still feel pain—but he does not quit. He may still be pressed—but he does not collapse. He may still be attacked—but he does not surrender.

Grace teaches the believer to stand in the storm without losing the fear of God, without losing holiness, and without losing hope.

And this endurance is not optional. The Christian life is a race. It is a fight. It is a narrow road. That is why grace is not decoration—it is fuel.

5) Grace Fuels the Inner Life: Prayer, Hunger, and Communion with God

A believer cannot live strong outwardly while dying inwardly. The secret place is not a luxury. It is life. And grace fuels the secret place.

When grace is flowing, prayer becomes less like duty and more like need. Hunger for the Word becomes real. Worship becomes living. Fellowship becomes necessary. Sin becomes repulsive. God becomes precious.

Grace fuels intimacy.

And when believers become dry, it is often because they have tried to live without drawing near. Grace is available, but it must be received. Not earned—received.

Grace does not only meet you in public worship; it meets you in the closet, in the Word, in confession, in surrender.

6) Grace Fuels Perseverance: Staying Faithful Until the End

This is where godly fear must remain: the Christian life is not merely starting—it is continuing.

Many are wounded today by a careless gospel that teaches people to treat salvation like a momentary contract rather than a living covenant. But Scripture calls believers to persevere, to abide, to endure, to hold fast.

Grace is what fuels perseverance. Grace supplies the strength to continue in faith when feelings fluctuate. Grace anchors the soul when trials shake you. Grace helps you resist deception. Grace keeps you sober in an age of compromise.

This is why Scripture warns:

"Looking carefully lest anyone fall short of the grace of God..."
(Hebrews 12:15, NKJV)

Falling short is not because God is unwilling to give grace. It is because the heart stops drawing near and begins to drift—neglecting prayer, neglecting the Word, ignoring conviction, tolerating sin, feeding the flesh, and calling it "grace."

Grace fuels perseverance, but the believer must not despise the fuel. The believer must not treat the supply as automatic while living careless.

7) A Deep Call to Godly Fear: Do Not Quench the Grace That Is Fueling You

Fuel can be resisted. The supply can be neglected. Grace can be received in vain. Grace can be insulted. Grace can be turned into a cloak for darkness. This is why fear of the Lord is a guardian of grace.

Beloved, if grace is fueling you, do not grieve the Spirit. Do not quiet conviction. Do not entertain what God has told you to cut off. Do not return to what Christ delivered you from.

Because when a believer begins to treat grace lightly, spiritual strength drains away—not because God is unfaithful, but because the believer is drifting from the very source of supply.

Grace is like fire: it warms the surrendered, but it exposes the rebellious. It strengthens the humble, but it resists the proud.

8) A Practical Picture: How to "Live Fueled by Grace" Daily

A life fueled by grace is marked by daily drawing near:

1. Daily surrender — "Lord, I am Yours today."

2. Daily Word — letting Scripture feed and correct you.

3. Daily prayer — receiving help before temptation conquers.

4. Daily repentance — quick confession, quick turning.

5. Daily resistance — shutting doors to the flesh.

6. Daily reliance — "Not I, but the grace of God with me."

7. Daily fear of the Lord — treasuring holiness, hating compromise.

This is not works-salvation. This is grace-sustained living.

Closing Scriptures for Meditation (NKJV)

- *"God is able to make all grace abound toward you... abundance for every good work." (2 Corinthians 9:8)*

- *"But by the grace of God... yet not I, but the grace of God which was with me." (1 Corinthians 15:10)*

- *"May the God of all grace... perfect, establish, strengthen, and settle you." (1 Peter 5:10)*

- *"Looking carefully lest anyone fall short of the grace of God..." (Hebrews 12:15)*

CHAPTER TEN:
GRACE IN PERSUASION
— THE WORD OF HIS
GRACE, BOLD WITNESS,
AND SPEECH THAT TURNS
HEARTS TO GOD

Grace does not only work in the believer. Grace also works through the believer.

One of the great tragedies of our time is that many Christians have reduced grace to something private—something that comforts them, helps them, sustains them—but never overflows into witness. Yet the God of grace never intended grace to end in you. Grace is a river. It flows into the redeemed so that it may flow out to the lost. Grace is given to save, to shape, to fuel—and to persuade.

This is why the early church was not timid. They were not silent. They were not ashamed. They did not treat the gospel as a personal opinion. They carried the message of grace as the only hope for humanity. And God Himself partnered with their witness.

Therefore they stayed there a long time, speaking boldly in the Lord, who was bearing witness to the word of His grace, granting signs and wonders to be done by their hands. (Acts 14:3, NKJV)

Notice what God calls the gospel: "the word of His grace."

And notice what the apostles did: they spoke boldly.

And notice what God did: He bore witness to that word.

Grace persuades through truth. Grace persuades through proclamation. Grace persuades by the Spirit convicting hearts. Grace persuades through grace-filled speech, grace-filled boldness, and grace-filled lives that testify that Jesus is real.

1) "The Word of His Grace" — The Gospel Is Grace Spoken

The gospel is not merely information. It is the proclamation of God's gracious rescue through Jesus Christ. When Scripture calls it "the word of His grace," it reveals that grace has a voice. Grace speaks. Grace calls. Grace confronts. Grace invites.

And the same God who pours grace into the heart pours grace into the mouth—so the believer speaks with clarity, authority, compassion, and fear of the Lord.

Many people think persuasion is manipulation. But biblical persuasion is not pressure. It is not emotional control. It is not clever speech designed to win arguments. Biblical persuasion is the Spirit of God using the truth of the gospel to awaken a dead soul.

When grace persuades, the heart becomes aware of sin, aware of judgment, aware of mercy, aware of Christ—and compelled to respond.

2) Boldness Is a Fruit of Grace, Not Personality

Acts 14:3 says they were "speaking boldly in the Lord." Boldness is not arrogance. Boldness is not aggression. Boldness is holy courage to speak truth when fear wants to silence you.

In Scripture, boldness is not presented as a personality trait; it is presented as a grace.

The apostles were not bold because they were naturally fearless. Many of them trembled, hid, and fled in the days of Christ's crucifixion. But when grace filled them—when the Spirit came—fear of man was broken.

Grace does this: it delivers you from the prison of human approval.

Grace makes eternity more real than embarrassment.

Grace makes the fear of the Lord greater than the fear of rejection.

And this is part of what it means to be fueled by grace: grace gives you a mouth that does not shrink back.

3) God Bears Witness When Grace Is Proclaimed

Acts 14:3 is stunning because it reveals a divine partnership:

- They spoke boldly.

- God bore witness.

This means the Lord Himself confirms the gospel message when it is preached in truth and in power. Sometimes He confirms it through conviction. Sometimes through miracles. Sometimes through deliverance. Sometimes through opened hearts. Sometimes through a sudden awareness of sin and the need for salvation.

But the point remains: when the word of grace is spoken, God is not passive. He is active.

This is why the enemy fights evangelism so fiercely. Because when grace is proclaimed, prisoners are set free. When grace is proclaimed, darkness loses ground. When grace is proclaimed, the kingdom of Satan is plundered.

4) Grace-Filled Speech: Truth with Tenderness and Fear of God

Grace in persuasion is not only public preaching. It is also daily speech—how believers speak in their homes, their workplaces, their families, their communities. Grace shapes the tongue.

The Spirit teaches believers not only what to say, but how to say it—without compromise, yet without fleshly harshness.

"Let your speech always be with grace, seasoned with salt, that you may know how you ought to answer each one." (Colossians 4:6, NKJV)

Grace-filled speech is:

- clean (no corruption)

- true (no flattery)

- bold (no cowardice)

- tender (no cruelty)

- serious (no joking about sin)

- wise (knowing when to speak and when to wait)

Grace does not water down truth, but it delivers truth with a heart that longs for repentance, not destruction.

5) Grace Persuades by Conviction: The Holy Spirit Exposes Sin with Mercy

Persuasion is not achieved merely by logic. Grace persuades by conviction. This is the mercy of God making sin visible—so the sinner can flee to Christ.

When a man laughs at sin, he is not free—he is blind. When a man justifies sin, he is not safe—he is deceived. So, conviction is mercy. It is grace's sharp edge cutting away deception.

This is why the believer must fear God: because a believer who softens sin in order to be "liked" is not moving in grace—he is moving in compromise. The word of grace must not be reshaped to fit the world. The gospel must remain the gospel: sin is real, judgment is real, Christ is the only Savior, and repentance is necessary.

Grace persuades by telling the truth plainly—then offering mercy fully.

6) Grace Persuades Through a Life That Matches the Message

Words without a holy life weaken persuasion. The world can sniff hypocrisy quickly. But when grace has truly shaped and fueled a believer, the believer becomes a living testimony. His purity convicts. His humility persuades. His repentance is real. His love is not fake. His fear of God is evident.

This does not mean perfection, but it means sincerity. It means a life in the light.

This is why godly fear matters: a believer who plays with sin while speaking of grace becomes a contradiction. But a believer who trembles at God's Word while proclaiming grace becomes powerful—because heaven backs the message.

7) A Deep Warning: Do Not Turn Persuasion Into Performance

There is a counterfeit "grace persuasion" that is manipulation—

smooth words without the cross, promises without repentance, comfort without holiness, "love" without truth.

But Acts 14:3 shows the apostles were speaking boldly "in the Lord." That means under His authority, for His glory, with His message—not their own.

So this chapter calls the reader to holy sobriety: speak the word of grace, but do not dilute it. Persuade, but do not manipulate. Invite, but do not flatter. Love souls, but do not remove the offense of the cross. The grace that saves is also the grace that calls men to repent.

8) A Call to the Reader: Become a Vessel of Grace Persuasion

Beloved, God did not save you to make you silent. He saved you to make you a witness. The grace that appeared to you is meant to appear through you—through your speech, your life, your courage, your prayers, your testimony.

Ask the Lord for this grace:

- grace to speak truth without fear

- grace to love souls without compromise

- grace to answer wisely

- grace to witness boldly

- grace to endure rejection

- grace to remain holy so your message carries weight

Because grace in persuasion is not a technique—it is a life surrendered to Christ, filled with the Spirit, and governed by the fear of the Lord.

Closing Scriptures for Meditation (NKJV)

- *"...speaking boldly in the Lord, who was bearing witness to the word of His grace..." (Acts 14:3)*

- *"Let your speech always be with grace..." (Colossians 4:6)*

- *"Or do you despise the riches of His goodness... leads you to repentance?" (Romans 2:4)*

CHAPTER ELEVEN: GRACE IN WAITING — THE HOLY STRENGTH TO ENDURE DELAY, SILENCE, AND TESTING WITHOUT DRIFTING INTO UNBELIEF

Waiting is one of the places where grace is proven.

Many believers can praise God when answers come quickly. Many can shout when doors open. Many can worship when the promise is in their hands. But when heaven is silent, when the answer delays, when the burden continues, when the season stretches longer than expected—that is when the soul is tested. Waiting reveals what is truly inside the heart: faith or presumption, humility or pride, surrender or control, reverence, or complaint.

And this is where we must go deeper: waiting is not the absence of grace. Waiting is one of grace's classrooms.

Grace does not only work in breakthrough; grace also works in delay. Grace does not only sustain the believer in victory; grace sustains the believer in process.

If you understand grace only as quick rescue, you will misinterpret waiting as rejection. But if you understand grace biblically, you will recognize that the same God who saves you by grace also trains you by grace, and waiting is part of that training.

1) Waiting Is Not Wasted When Grace Is Working

One of the greatest lies the enemy whispers in seasons of delay is: "Nothing is happening."

But waiting does not mean God is idle. It often means God is doing a deeper work than the one you asked for. You may be praying for a change in circumstance while God is forming Christ in you. You may be asking for an open door while God is strengthening your inner man to walk through it without pride. You may be asking for the promise while God is preparing your character to carry it without falling into sin.

The Lord is not only concerned with what He gives you. He is concerned with who you become.

This is why grace in waiting is precious: it keeps you from rushing ahead of God and building an Ishmael with religious impatience. It protects you from grabbing what looks good but is not ordained. It delivers you from murmuring, from bitterness, from spiritual fatigue, and from compromise.

2) Grace in Waiting Sustains Faith When Feelings Fade

Waiting is dangerous because feelings change. In waiting, the believer can move from hope to frustration, from worship to complaint, from confidence to suspicion.

But grace sustains faith when emotions fluctuate. Grace keeps the heart anchored to God's character—not to circumstances.

We are not sustained by visible evidence alone; the Word of God sustains us. Grace trains the believer to say:

- "Even if I do not see it yet, God is faithful."

- "Even if I feel weak, God's grace is sufficient."

- "Even if the promise delays, God does not lie."

This is the holy work of grace in waiting: it teaches the believer to walk by faith, not by sight.

3) Waiting Exposes the Flesh—So Grace Can Crucify It

Let's go deeper: the flesh hates waiting.

The flesh wants control. The flesh wants immediate relief. The flesh wants answers now. The flesh becomes irritated when it cannot manipulate the outcome. This is why waiting becomes a battlefield between surrender and self-will.

Grace in waiting does not merely help you "cope." It begins to crucify the old nature. It breaks the need to control. It breaks the spirit of entitlement. It breaks the demand that God must operate on your timeline.

And here is where godly fear must govern the heart: a believer who grows impatient in waiting can become vulnerable to sin—compromise, bitterness, unbelief, murmuring, resentment, or seeking counterfeit comfort.

Waiting is where some believers fall—not because God failed them, but because they refused the discipline of grace.

4) Grace in Waiting Keeps the Heart Tender and Repentant

Seasons of delay can harden the heart. When answers don't come, some begin to accuse God in their spirit. Some become cynical. Some stop praying. Some stop trusting. Some begin to tolerate sin to "feel better," and then call it "stress."

But grace in waiting keeps the heart tender. Grace keeps repentance close. Grace teaches the believer to examine himself in silence, to confess quickly, to remain clean, to maintain a pure conscience.

This is where the fear of the Lord becomes a guardian: it keeps the believer from turning waiting into spiritual numbness.

"Looking carefully lest anyone fall short of the grace of God..."
(Hebrews 12:15, NKJV)

How does a believer fall short? Often by drifting in waiting—neglecting prayer, neglecting the Word, allowing bitterness to take root, allowing discouragement to become unbelief.

Grace in waiting is God preventing that drift.

5) Grace in Waiting Produces Patience That Is Holy Strength

Patience is not passivity. Patience is not laziness. Patience is holy endurance under God.

There is a worldly patience that is resignation: "Nothing matters."

And there is a biblical patience that is strength: "God is faithful; I will not move without Him."

Grace produces this kind of patience—because patience is not natural to fallen man. Patience is a fruit of the Spirit and a product of grace.

Grace teaches the believer to endure without complaining, to continue without quitting, to worship without seeing, to obey without feeling, and to remain faithful until God moves.

6) Grace in Waiting Protects the Promise by Preparing the Vessel

Many want the promise, but few want the preparation.

But Scripture reveals a pattern: God often delays the gift to deepen the vessel. Not because He enjoys withholding, but because He is wise. He knows what the promise will require. He knows what the blessing will expose. He knows what new levels of favor will demand.

So, grace in waiting does this:

- It teaches humility before promotion.

- It teaches obedience before authority.

- It teaches purity before increase.

- It teaches dependence before expansion.

Waiting is not rejection. Waiting is refinement.

7) A Sobering Word: Waiting Can Become a Door to Unbelief If Grace Is Despised

Here is where we must speak with godly fear: some believers lose their spiritual edge in waiting.

Not because God stopped being gracious—but because they stopped drawing near. The longer the delay, the more they loosen their grip on the Word. They begin to entertain doubt. They begin to murmur. They begin to seek comfort in the flesh. They begin to justify compromise: "God understands."

Beloved, God does understand—but grace is not given to excuse compromise. Grace is given to prevent compromise.

Waiting is not the time to relax spiritually; it is the time to become watchful. Waiting is where prayer must deepen, not disappear. Waiting is where the Word must become bread, not background noise.

Grace in waiting is the difference between a believer who becomes bitter and a believer who becomes mature.

8) How to Live in Grace While Waiting (Practical Holy Posture)

If you are in a waiting season, grace calls you to a posture:

1. Remain in the Word — let promise and truth feed you daily.

2. Pray honestly — pour out your heart without accusation.

3. Repent quickly — keep the conscience clean.

4. Reject murmuring — don't let complaint become your language.

5. Stay obedient — do not pause obedience until the answer comes.

6. Worship in the silence — because God is worthy even in delay.

7. Guard your heart — bitterness is a root; do not let it grow.

Grace doesn't only help you wait—it teaches you to wait in a way that honors God.

Closing Exhortation: Let Waiting Make You Holy, Not Hardened

Beloved, do not waste your waiting.

Let waiting make you pure.

Let waiting make you prayerful.

Let waiting make you humble.

Let waiting make you sober.

Let waiting make you hungry for God.

Let waiting make you more like Christ.

Because the grace of God is not only unquenchable in breakthrough—it is unquenchable in delay. And if you will yield to it, waiting will not destroy you. It will establish you.

Closing Scriptures for Meditation (NKJV)

- *"My grace is sufficient for you..." (2 Corinthians 12:9)*

- *"Looking carefully lest anyone fall short of the grace of God..." (Hebrews 12:15)*

- *"The grace of God... teaching us..." (Titus 2:11–12)*

CHAPTER TWELVE: GRACE IN HEALING — THE MERCY THAT RESTORES THE BROKEN, AND THE HOLY POWER THAT CALLS THE HEALED TO REPENTANCE

(Going Deeper: Healing as Covenant Kindness, Not Entitlement)

There is a kind of pain that the human body carries, and there is a kind of pain the soul carries—quiet wounds, hidden bruises, unresolved grief, cycles of fear, shame, rejection, trauma, condemnation, and inward torment that people learn to smile through while dying inside.

And many believers, when they hear the word healing, think only of the body. But the grace of God is deeper than muscles and bones. The grace of God reaches into marrow and memory, into conscience and craving, into the tears you never explained and the battles you never told anyone about.

Grace in healing is not merely God making you feel better.

Grace in healing is God restoring you to wholeness—so you may belong to Him fully.

And this chapter must begin with a holy truth: God is compassionate. He is not distant from suffering. He is not indifferent to pain. He is the Father of mercies, the God who binds up the brokenhearted, the One who heals—not only to relieve pain, but to reveal Himself.

Yet here is where we must go deeper and keep godly fear: healing grace must never be treated as entitlement. God heals because He is merciful, not because we control Him. God heals because He is good, not because we deserve it. And when He heals, He calls the healed to holiness—because healing is not merely restoration of the body; it is restoration of the heart.

1) Healing Is an Expression of Grace, Not a Reward for Perfection

Many believers struggle because they think healing must be earned. They assume God heals only the "strong," only the "pure," only those who have never failed. But Jesus shattered that lie repeatedly. He healed the broken, the rejected, the unclean, the weary, the desperate.

When grace heals, it is God saying, "I am merciful, and I am near."

And yet, we must also say with reverence: healing is not proof that a person is right with God. People can experience healing and still remain unconverted if they refuse repentance. Healing is grace, but salvation is greater grace. Healing is mercy in time, but reconciliation is mercy for eternity.

This is why healing must point the heart to Christ—not away from Him.

2) Healing Grace Flows from the Nature of God: He Is the Lord Who Heals

In Scripture, God reveals Himself as healer—not as a slogan, but as identity.

"I am the LORD who heals you." (Exodus 15:26, NKJV)

This is not merely physical. It is covenanting language. It means God is the One who restores what is broken. Sin broke humanity. The fall fractured the inner man. And God's redemptive heart includes restoration.

But let's go deeper: God heals in a way that protects His glory. He heals so that the healed will know Him, fear Him, and walk with Him—not so they can return to sin with a stronger body and the same rebellious heart.

3) The Greatest Healing Is the Healing of the Heart (Because Sin Is the Deepest Disease)

There is a reason Jesus often dealt with sin while dealing with sickness. Not because sickness is always caused by personal sin—but because the deepest sickness of humanity is separation from God.

When Jesus healed the paralytic, He first spoke words that shocked everyone:

"Son, your sins are forgiven you." (Mark 2:5, NKJV)

Then He healed the body. Why? Because Jesus was revealing priority: forgiveness and restoration to God is greater than temporary bodily strength. A man can be healed and still be lost. A man can be forgiven and still be physically weak—but eternally saved.

Grace in healing is meant to bring the whole person back into alignment with God.

4) Healing Grace and Repentance: Jesus' Warning to the Healed

Here is a passage many ignore, but it is necessary for godly fear. After Jesus healed a man who had been sick for thirty-eight years, He later found him and said:

"See, you have been made well. Sin no more, lest a worse thing come upon you." (John 5:14, NKJV)

This is not cruel. This is mercy with teeth. This is healing grace speaking with holy seriousness.

Jesus did not only heal him—He warned him. Why? Because grace that heals must not become grace that is abused. God restores, and then He calls the restored to holiness.

This is the dimension many want to avoid: they want healing without surrender. They want restoration without repentance. But the Lord loves too deeply to heal you and leave you enslaved.

Grace heals—and grace also calls you to walk clean.

5) "Time for Grace": Healing Is Not Always Instant, but Grace Is Always Present

Some believers are healed instantly. Others are healed through a process. Others endure affliction for a season. The danger is that people interpret delay as absence of grace. But grace is not absent in process; grace is present in weakness.

"My grace is sufficient for you..." (2 Corinthians 12:9, NKJV)

Here is the deeper truth: sometimes God heals by removing the sickness; sometimes He heals by strengthening the soul through it; sometimes He heals by delivering the heart from fear, bitterness, and despair while the body still fights.

This is still healing—because a tormented heart is a sickness too.

Grace is not only the miracle at the end. Grace is also the sustaining presence in the middle.

6) Healing Grace Restores the Soul: Shame, Trauma, Fear, and the Inner Wounds

Many believers carry hidden sickness:

- shame from past sin

- condemnation from failure

- fear that controls decision-making

- trauma that keeps the mind in bondage

- bitterness that poisons relationships

- rejection that shapes identity

This is where grace becomes a holy surgeon. It cuts out lies, heals memories, breaks strongholds, restores identity, and renews the mind.

And this kind of healing often requires humility and repentance—not because you "earned" it, but because healing requires you to bring the wound into the light. You cannot be healed in what you refuse to expose.

Grace invites the believer to confess, to forgive, to release, to surrender—and to be made whole.

7) Healing Grace Must Not Become a Marketplace

Now we must speak plainly: The spirit of religion often abuses the grace of healing. People turn healing into performance, into profit, into manipulation, into emotional excitement. But grace does not merchandise the suffering.

Grace is holy. Healing is sacred. The weak are not a stage.

The Lord is not impressed by noise. He is not moved by theatrics. He is honored by faith, humility, obedience, and reverence.

Grace in healing must bring glory to Christ—not glory to a man, a ministry, or a method.

8) A Deep Warning: Being Healed Is Not the Same as Being Changed

This must provoke godly fear: Jesus healed many, but not all followed Him. Ten lepers were cleansed, but only one returned to give thanks (Luke 17). That story is a mirror of the human heart: people love relief, but they may resist lordship.

So, healing must never become the end goal. Jesus is the end goal.

If God heals you, do not return to sin with a testimony on your lips and compromise in your life. Do not take the mercy and then despise the One who gave it. Do not receive grace and then receive it "in vain."

Let healing become a doorway into deeper consecration.

9) How to Respond to Healing Grace (A Holy Posture)

If you are seeking healing, or if you have received healing, respond with reverence:

1. Come to Christ first — not just to relief.

2. Examine the heart — ask the Spirit to search you.

3. Repent quickly — sin no more; cut off compromise.

4. Forgive — bitterness can keep wounds open.

5. Ask in faith — but submit to God's wisdom.

6.   Give thanks — gratitude guards you from entitlement.

7.   Walk in holiness — healing is not permission; it is stewardship.

Closing Exhortation: Let Healing Become Consecration

Beloved, the Lord heals because He is gracious. But the grace that heals is also the grace that sanctifies. If He restores your strength, it is not so you can live for yourself. If He lifts your burden, it is not so you can return to bondage. If He touches your body or soul, it is to draw you nearer—to make you whole, clean, and faithful.

So let healing grace do its full work:

Heal me, Lord—

and make me holy.

Restore me—

and keep me tender.

Deliver me—

and teach me to fear You.

Strengthen me—

and let me never take Your grace for granted.

Closing Scriptures for Meditation (NKJV)

* *"I am the LORD who heals you." (Exodus 15:26)*

* *"See, you have been made well. Sin no more..." (John 5:14)*

* *"My grace is sufficient for you..." (2 Corinthians 12:9)*

* *"Is anyone among you sick? Let him call for the elders..." (James 5:14–16)*

CHAPTER THIRTEEN: GRACE IN OBTAINING THE PROMISES OF GOD — INHERITED BY FAITH AND PATIENCE, PROTECTED BY GODLY FEAR

There are promises in Scripture that make the heart burn—promises of salvation, sanctification, provision, deliverance, wisdom, fruitfulness, answered prayer, protection, peace, and eternal glory. God has not left His people without hope. He has spoken. He has pledged. He has covenanted. He has promised.

And yet, many believers live as though the promises of God are distant—always "someday," always out of reach, always delayed. Some become discouraged. Some grow bitter. Some drift into unbelief. Some attempt to force the promise with fleshly methods. Some compromise.

Some even abandon faith altogether.

This is why we must go deeper: the promises of God are obtained by grace. Not by human striving, not by religious pressure, not by manipulation—but by the grace of God empowering faith, patience, obedience, and perseverance.

And grace must also produce godly fear: because promises can be forfeited through unbelief, disobedience, hardness of heart, and idolatry. God is faithful—but we must not treat His faithfulness as permission to live carelessly.

1) God's Promises Are Not Wages — They Are Covenant Grace

A promise is not a paycheck. A promise is not earned like wages. A promise flows from God's covenant heart. God promises because He is faithful—because He cannot lie—because He delights in showing mercy.

"For all the promises of God in Him are Yes, and in Him Amen, to the glory of God through us." (2 Corinthians 1:20, NKJV)

Notice: "in Him." The promises are anchored in Christ. They are not anchored in your performance; they are anchored in His Person. But this does not remove responsibility; it reveals the true pathway: abide in Christ and walk in faith.

Grace is the foundation of the promise, and faith is the means of receiving it.

2) Promises Are Inherited — Through Faith and Patience

Scripture gives a simple, sobering principle:

"...do not become sluggish, but imitate those who through faith and patience inherit the promises." (Hebrews 6:12, NKJV)

This verse destroys two extremes:

- It destroys spiritual laziness ("I'll just wait and do nothing").

- And it destroys fleshly striving ("I'll force it in my own strength").

Promises are inherited through faith and patience. Faith believes God is true. Patience endures until the appointed time. Grace fuels both—because faith and patience are not sustained by human willpower alone. They are sustained by grace.

Grace is what keeps faith alive in the waiting.

Grace is what keeps patience from turning into bitterness.

3) Grace Protects the Heart in Delay — So Unbelief Doesn't Take Root

Many believers do not lose promises because God changed His mind. They lose promises because the heart becomes hardened.

The writer of Hebrews warns believers with holy seriousness:

"Beware, brethren, lest there be in any of you an evil heart of unbelief in departing from the living God." (Hebrews 3:12, NKJV)

Unbelief is not always loud. Often it begins as quiet discouragement—then complaint—then cynicism—then spiritual numbness—then withdrawal—then compromise.

And this is why grace in obtaining promises must be joined to godly fear: fear of drifting, fear of hardening, fear of despising the Lord's patience, fear of treating delay as permission to sin.

Grace sustains the believer so that delay becomes refinement rather than rebellion.

4) The Wilderness Warning: Promises Can Be Near Yet Not Entered

Israel had a promise—Canaan. Yet an entire generation did not enter.

Not because the promise was false, but because unbelief and disobedience prevailed.

This is written for our instruction.

"So, we see that they could not enter in because of unbelief." (Hebrews 3:19, NKJV)

This should awaken godly fear in every believer who takes grace lightly. The promise can be proclaimed and still not possessed. The inheritance can be offered and still refused. The door can be open and still not entered.

Why? Because unbelief is not merely "doubt." Unbelief is a heart posture that refuses to trust and obey God.

Grace is given to destroy that posture—to create a heart that clings to God with reverence.

5) Grace and Obedience: Many Promises Are Attached to Walking in God's Ways

We must speak plainly: while salvation is by grace through faith apart from works, many promises concerning fruitfulness, protection, intimacy, and spiritual authority are attached to obedience—because obedience is the pathway where God's blessing rests.

This is not works-salvation. This is covenant order.

Jesus said:

"If you abide in Me, and My words abide in you, you will ask what you desire, and it shall be done for you." (John 15:7, NKJV)

"Abide." That is covenant language. Abiding is obedience, surrender, staying in fellowship, staying in the light, remaining in Christ. Many believers want the promise without abiding—but Scripture will not separate them.

Grace gives you the power to abide. Grace gives you the strength to obey. Grace gives you the fear of God to refuse compromise.

6) The Enemy Fights Promises — So Grace Gives Power to Stand

Whenever God speaks a promise, warfare intensifies. The devil fears what God has pledged over your life because the promise reveals God's intention. So, the enemy attacks through:

- delay to produce discouragement

- temptation to produce compromise

- deception to produce unbelief

- offense to produce bitterness

- distractions to produce spiritual dullness

This is why grace is necessary to obtain promises: grace strengthens the believer in warfare, so he does not abandon the path.

And here is the deeper truth: the promise is not only what God will give you; the promise is also what God will make you. Often the greatest promise is not the thing—it is the formation of Christ within you.

7) "Time for Grace" — God's Timing Is Part of the Promise

Promises have timing. God's promises are not merely true; they are also appointed.

Delay is not denial. But delay is dangerous to the flesh because it tests motives: Do you want God, or do you want what God gives?

Grace in obtaining promises teaches the believer to worship God in the waiting, obey God in the silence, and trust God when nothing moves.

And while you wait, grace keeps you clean, humble, and tender.

8) A Deep Call to Godly Fear: Do Not Forfeit Promises Through Sin and Idolatry

Now we must speak with seriousness: sin can derail the promise—especially willful sin, unbelief, and idolatry.

Not because God's Word is weak, but because sin hardens the heart, grieves the Spirit, and opens doors to deception. Many have exchanged God's promise for temporary pleasure. Many have traded inheritance for appetite, like Esau. Many have compromised and then wondered why their spiritual life became dry.

Grace is given to protect you from that exchange. Grace empowers you to say no. Grace strengthens you to endure. Grace teaches you to fear the Lord more than you desire immediate gratification.

This is why Scripture warns:

"Looking carefully lest anyone fall short of the grace of God..."
(Hebrews 12:15, NKJV)

Falling short often looks like forfeiting what God intended—because the heart stopped taking God seriously.

9) How to Obtain Promises by Grace (Practical Steps Without Legalism)

To inherit promises through grace, the believer must live in posture:

1. Anchor in Scripture — know what God promised.

2. Ask in faith — not doubting God's character.

3. Walk in obedience — keep your conscience clean.

4. Practice patience — refuse murmuring; refuse despair.

5.   Resist temptation — do not trade promise for pleasure.

6.   Stay in fellowship — isolation breeds unbelief.

7.   Give thanks — gratitude protects the heart.

8.   Wait for God's timing — do not force doors.

9.   Keep godly fear — the promise is holy; your life must be holy.

Closing Exhortation: Let Grace Make You an Heir Who Endures

Beloved, the promises of God are real. They are "Yes" in Christ. But they are inherited through faith and patience. And grace is what fuels both.

Do not become sluggish.

Do not drift into unbelief.

Do not allow bitterness to grow.

Do not compromise under pressure.

Do not force what God has not released.

Instead, let grace do its work: strengthen you, establish you, keep you holy, and bring you into the promises at the appointed time—so God receives the glory, and your life becomes a testimony.

Closing Scriptures for Meditation (NKJV)

- *"...through faith and patience inherit the promises." (Hebrews 6:12)*

- *"Beware, brethren, lest there be... an evil heart of unbelief..." (Hebrews 3:12)*

- *"So, we see that they could not enter in because of unbelief." (Hebrews 3:19)*

- *"For all the promises of God in Him are Yes…" (2 Corinthians 1:20)*

CHAPTER FOURTEEN: THE GIFTS OF GOD BY HIS GRACE — GRACE THAT DISTRIBUTES POWER, YET DEMANDS HOLINESS

(Deeper Revelation: Gifted Does Not Mean Approved)

One of the most misunderstood realities in the church is this: God can gift a man more than that man has been sanctified.

God can anoint a vessel whose character still needs deep purification.

God can use a believer in power while that believer still needs deliverance from pride, hidden sin, or spiritual immaturity.

This is not because God is careless. It is because gifts are an expression of grace, not a reward for perfection. The Lord gives gifts because He loves His people and because He is building His Church. But because gifts come by grace, they can be abused. And because they can be abused, the fear of the Lord must return to the topic of spiritual gifts.

If we do not understand this, we will confuse gifting with godliness, and power with purity—and many will be deceived.

This chapter is written to restore both wonder and trembling: wonder at the generosity of God, and trembling at the responsibility of carrying His gifts.

1) Gifts Are Grace in Motion: Not Earned, Not Bought, Not Deserved

Spiritual gifts are not wages. They are not medals. They are not trophies for spiritual achievement. Scripture says they are distributed by the Spirit according to His will.

"But the manifestation of the Spirit is given to each one for the profit of all... But one and the same Spirit works all these things, distributing to each one individually as He wills." (1 Corinthians 12:7, 11, NKJV)

And Paul ties gifts directly to grace:

"Having then gifts differing according to the grace that is given to us, let us use them..." (Romans 12:6, NKJV)

That phrase "according to the grace" means the gift is not the product of your merit—it is the product of God's generosity. Grace is the source. The gift is the expression.

So, no man can boast. No ministry can claim ownership. No believer can say, "This is mine." Gifts are entrusted, not possessed.

2) Grace Gives Gifts for a Purpose: "For the Profit of All"

Gifts are not primarily given for platform—they are given for people. Not for fame, but for edification. Not for self-exaltation, but for the building up of the body of Christ.

"The manifestation of the Spirit is given to each one for the profit of all." (1 Corinthians 12:7, NKJV)

Grace gives gifts to heal, strengthen, teach, warn, comfort, equip, and mature the saints. A gift that is used for self-glory is no longer operating under grace; it is being hijacked by the flesh.

This is why Godly fear is essential: gifts are not toys. They are holy trusts.

3) The Deeper Revelation: Gifts Can Operate Without Mature Character

Here is the revelation that must sober the church: gifts can be present where holiness is lacking.

The Corinthian church flowed in gifts—tongues, prophecy, knowledge—yet they were carnally divided, morally compromised, and spiritually immature. Paul did not deny their gifting. He rebuked their carnality.

"Now you are the body of Christ, and members individually." (1 Corinthians 12:27, NKJV)

(Then Paul corrects their disorder and sin throughout the letter.)

This means it is possible to be gifted and yet:

- proud

- divisive

- lustful

- greedy

- prayerless

- unforgiving

- manipulative

- spiritually immature

And because this is possible, it is also possible for people to be impressed by power and ignore fruit. But heaven is not impressed by gifts alone—heaven looks for Christlike character.

This is why Jesus warned that some will prophesy and do miracles and still be rejected:

"Many will say to Me in that day, 'Lord, Lord, have we not prophesied in Your name... and done many wonders in Your name?' And then I will declare to them, 'I never knew you; depart from Me, you who practice lawlessness!'" (Matthew 7:22–23, NKJV)

This is terrifying. It means miracles are not the definitive evidence of intimacy. Works are not the ultimate proof of knowing Christ. Holiness matters. Obedience matters. Lawlessness disqualifies.

So let godly fear settle in the reader: do not measure your life by gifting. Measure it by fruit.

4) The Difference Between Gift and Fruit: Grace Gives Gifts, Grace Produces Fruit

Gifts are given by grace. Fruit is produced by abiding.

Gifts can be received quickly. Fruit takes time.

Gifts can function through the anointing. Fruit reveals the nature.

Gifts can impress people. Fruit pleases God.

Paul makes this distinction unavoidable in 1 Corinthians 13—right in the middle of the gifts chapters:

"Though I speak with the tongues of men and of angels... and have prophecy... and understand all mysteries... and have all faith... but

have not love, I am nothing." (1 Corinthians 13:1–2, NKJV)

Love is fruit. Love is Christlikeness. Love is the evidence of grace shaping the heart.

So here is the deeper revelation: it is possible to have gifts and still be "nothing" in God's eyes if the heart is not being transformed.

This is not to condemn the gifted—it is to call the gifted to holiness.

5) Gifts Are Not Permission to Live Carelessly — They Increase Accountability

The more God entrusts to a believer, the more serious that believer's stewardship becomes. Gifts are grace, but they are also responsibility. They carry weight.

If God gives you a gift of teaching, you must fear God with your tongue.

If God gives you prophecy, you must fear God with accuracy and humility.

If God gives you influence, you must fear God with purity.

If God gives you healing, you must fear God and never merchandise mercy.

If God gives you leadership, you must fear God and never dominate people.

Grace does not remove accountability; it increases it—because to whom much is given, much is required.

6) Grace Gives Gifts, but Grace Also Trains the Gifted

Titus 2:11–12 must govern gifts:

"For the grace of God... teaching us that, denying ungodliness... we

should live soberly, righteously, and godly…" (Titus 2:11–12, NKJV)

The same grace that gives gifts also trains the vessel. If a believer celebrates gifts but resists training, that believer is heading toward deception.

Because gifts without holiness become a doorway to pride.

Gifts without purity become a doorway to sexual sin.

Gifts without humility become a doorway to manipulation.

Gifts without fear of God become a doorway to spiritual ruin.

Grace will gift you, yes—but grace will also confront you.

7) The Gifts of Grace Are Also "Callings" — You Don't Choose Them, You Respond to Them

Another deeper dimension: gifts are not merely abilities, they are often connected to calling. Grace assigns function in the body.

"And He Himself gave some to be apostles, some prophets, some evangelists, and some pastors and teachers…" (Ephesians 4:11, NKJV)

These are grace-gifts to the Church. They are not titles to chase; they are burdens to carry. They are not crowns; they are crosses. True calling humbles a man. True calling drives a man to prayer. True calling makes a man tremble because he knows: this is God's work, not mine.

8) A Deep Warning for the End Times: Many Will Follow Power Without Truth

In the last days, Scripture warns that deception will increase—signs, wonders, and persuasive spiritual experiences will mislead many. Therefore, believers must learn to test.

Power must be tested by truth.

Anointing must be tested by obedience.

Gifts must be tested by doctrine.

Experience must be tested by Scripture.

Grace does not call us to be naive. Grace calls us to be discerning.

9) The Holy Way to Walk in Gifts: Trembling, Love, and Purity

If you desire gifts, desire them rightly. If you have gifts, steward them rightly.

A grace-filled, fear-governed approach looks like this:

1.   Stay hidden with God — intimacy must exceed ministry.

2.   Walk in repentance — keep your conscience tender.

3.   Pursue holiness — gifts are not a substitute for purity.

4.   Serve the body — gifts are for others, not ego.

5.   Refuse merchandise — don't sell what grace gives freely.

6.   Submit to correction — the gifted need accountability.

7.   Remain humble — always remember: it is grace.

Closing Exhortation: Let Grace Make You Holy, Not Just Gifted

Beloved, the Church does not only need gifted people. The Church needs holy people. The world does not need spiritual performers. The world needs witnesses—men and women who tremble at God's Word, walk in purity, and carry the gifts of grace with humility and love.

May God deliver us from the deception of measuring spirituality by power alone. And may God raise up a remnant who carry His gifts with trembling hands—because they fear Him, love Him, and refuse to take His grace for granted.

Closing Scriptures for Meditation (NKJV)

- *"Having then gifts differing according to the grace that is given to us…" (Romans 12:6)*

- *"The manifestation of the Spirit is given to each one for the profit of all…" (1 Corinthians 12:7)*

- *"…distributing to each one individually as He wills." (1 Corinthians 12:11)*

- *"Many will say… have we not… done many wonders…? …I never knew you…" (Matthew 7:22–23)*

- *"The grace of God… teaching us… denying ungodliness…" (Titus 2:11–12)*

CHAPTER FOURTEEN: (CONTINUED) THE NINE GIFTS OF THE SPIRIT — GRACE MANIFESTED FOR THE EDIFICATION OF THE BODY

(Going Deeper: What They Are, How They Operate, and Why Godly Fear Must Guard Them)

If we are going to speak of the gifts of God by His grace, we must not remain general. The Holy Spirit did not leave the Church with vague language. He named the manifestations. He revealed their purpose. He gave boundaries for order. And He anchored everything in love—because gifts without love become noise, and power without holiness becomes a snare.

The nine gifts (or manifestations) of the Spirit are not toys for spiritual excitement. They are not badges of superiority. They are not spiritual entertainment. They are grace in operation—the living God working through human vessels for the profit of all.

"But the manifestation of the Spirit is given to each one for the profit of all." (1 Corinthians 12:7, NKJV)

That word manifestation matters. It means the Spirit makes Himself known—He shows Himself, expresses Himself, reveals Himself, empowers Himself—through His people. It is not your power. It is not your glory. It is not your possession. It is the Spirit manifesting.

And the Spirit lists these nine:

"To one is given the word of wisdom through the Spirit, to another the word of knowledge through the same Spirit, to another faith by the same Spirit, to another gifts of healings by the same Spirit, to another the working of miracles, to another prophecy, to another discerning of spirits, to another different kinds of tongues, to another the interpretation of tongues." (1 Corinthians 12:8–10, NKJV)

Let's go deeper—with trembling.

1) The Foundation: Gifts Flow from Grace, and Grace Demands Reverence

Before we expound each gift, we must build the foundation the Bible builds:

1. The gifts are distributed by the Spirit, not controlled by men. "But one and the same Spirit works all these things, distributing to each one individually as He wills." (1 Corinthians 12:11, NKJV)

2. The gifts are for edification, not self-exaltation. "Let all things be done for edification." (1 Corinthians 14:26, NKJV)

3. The gifts must be governed by love, or they become spiritual noise.

   "Though I speak with the tongues of men and of angels, but have not love, I have become sounding brass or a clanging cymbal." (1 Corinthians 13:1, NKJV)

4. The gifts must be governed by holiness, or the vessel becomes dangerous.

   "Pursue love, and desire spiritual gifts…" (1 Corinthians 14:1, NKJV)

   (Notice: pursue love first, then desire gifts—love is the guardrail.)

This is why godly fear must return: gifts are holy, and mishandling holy things invites judgment and deception.

2) The Nine Gifts Grouped for Clarity

(Three categories many teachers use, helpful for understanding)

A) Revelation Gifts (God reveals something)

- Word of Wisdom

- Word of Knowledge

- Discerning of Spirits

B) Power Gifts (God empowers something)

- Faith (special faith)

- Gifts of Healings

- Working of Miracles

C) Utterance Gifts (God speaks something)

- Prophecy

- Different Kinds of Tongues

- Interpretation of Tongues

These categories are not Scripture's "official headings," but they help the reader see how the Spirit moves: revelation, power, utterance—all for Christ's glory.

REVELATION GIFTS

3) The Word of Wisdom

What it is

A Spirit-given fragment of wisdom—direction, strategy, or insight about what to do, often concerning the future or a divine plan. It is not general wisdom from life experience. It is not merely good advice. It is God giving precision.

What it does

- Gives guidance when human wisdom is insufficient

- Reveals divine timing ("now" vs "not yet")

- Provides strategy in warfare, ministry, decision-making

- Prevents traps and preserves lives

Godly fear guardrail

Never call your opinion "Thus says the Lord." The word of wisdom is holy. False claims damage souls. The vessel must tremble.

"If any of you lacks wisdom, let him ask of God..." (James 1:5, NKJV)

(We ask; He gives. But when it is a manifestation gift, it comes with supernatural precision.)

4) The Word of Knowledge

What it is

A Spirit-revealed fact—something you could not know naturally. It may expose hidden conditions, reveal a person's need, uncover a root issue, or bring clarity for healing and deliverance.

What it does

- Brings conviction to sinners (God sees)

- Helps identify sickness or spiritual bondage for ministry

- Strengthens faith ("God knows me… God is present")

- Confirms God's guidance

Godly fear guardrail

Word of knowledge is not permission to embarrass people. It must be handled with mercy, confidentiality, and love. The goal is restoration, not exposure for display.

"And there is no creature hidden from His sight…" (Hebrews 4:13, NKJV)

When God reveals, He does it like a Surgeon—precise, healing, purposeful.

5) Discerning of Spirits

What it is

A supernatural ability to distinguish what spirit is operating: the Holy Spirit, a human spirit (flesh/soul), or demonic spirits. This is not suspicion. This is not cynicism. This is not personality-based "discernment." It is a gift.

What it does

- Protects the Church from deception

- Exposes false prophecy, false teachers, false manifestations

- Helps deliverance ministry (identifying demonic oppression)

- Helps leaders guard doctrine and purity

Godly fear guardrail

This gift must not become a weapon of accusation. Many have wounded the body by calling everything "a demon" or by being spiritually paranoid. True discernment is sober, humble, scriptural, and accountable.

"Beloved, do not believe every spirit, but test the spirits…" (1 John 4:1, NKJV)

Discerning of spirits helps the Church obey this command without guessing.

POWER GIFTS

6) Faith (Special Faith)

What it is

This is not saving faith (everyone must have that). This is not everyday faith (we all walk by faith). This is a supernatural surge of God-confidence—the Spirit giving an unshakable certainty that God will do something.

What it does

- Produces bold action (risk-taking obedience)

- Stands firm when circumstances scream "impossible"

- Releases miracles and deliverance

- Strengthens others' faith

Godly fear guardrail

Special faith must never become presumption. Presumption forces God; faith obeys God. Presumption boasts, faith trembles.

"Now faith is the substance of things hoped for…" (Hebrews 11:1, NKJV)

When the Spirit gives this gift, it becomes a weapon against fear.

7) Gifts of Healings

What it is

Notice the plural: gifts of healings. The Spirit may heal in diverse ways, for diverse conditions, in diverse moments. Healing is an expression of Christ's compassion and kingdom power.

What it does

- Heals bodies (sickness, disease, pain)

- Restores mental/emotional affliction (as God wills)

- Confirms the gospel with mercy

- Strengthens faith and awakens hearts

Godly fear guardrail

Healing must never be merchandised, staged, or used to build a man's name. The glory belongs to Christ. And the healed must be pointed to repentance and discipleship, not just testimony.

"And these signs will follow those who believe… they will lay hands on the sick, and they will recover." (Mark 16:17–18, NKJV)

8) Working of Miracles

What it is

Miracles are works of power beyond healing—supernatural intervention in circumstances, nature, provision, deliverance, or impossible situations. Healing repairs what is broken; miracles often override natural law.

What it does

- Delivers from danger

- Breaks chains and demonic oppression

- Provides supernaturally

- Confirms God's authority over creation

Godly fear guardrail

Miracles must never replace Scripture as the foundation. Signs follow truth; they do not define truth. And the Church must beware of end-times deception—where lying signs can mislead the undiscerning.

"For false christs and false prophets will rise and show great signs and wonders..." (Matthew 24:24, NKJV)

Therefore, miracles must be tested by doctrine and fruit.

UTTERANCE GIFTS

9) Prophecy

What it is

Prophecy is Spirit-inspired utterance in a known language that strengthens the Church. In the New Testament context, prophecy primarily serves:

- edification

- exhortation

- comfort

"But he who prophesies speaks edification and exhortation and comfort to men." (1 Corinthians 14:3, NKJV)

Prophecy may sometimes include predictive elements, but it is not primarily fortune-telling. It is God speaking to build His people.

Godly fear guardrail

Prophecy must be weighed and tested. The prophet is not above correction. God is not honored by reckless words spoken in His name.

"Let two or three prophets speak, and let the others judge." (1 Corinthians 14:29, NKJV)

Judging here means weighing—not condemning—testing for alignment with Scripture and the Spirit.

10) Different Kinds of Tongues

What it is

Tongues are Spirit-enabled utterance in a language unknown to the speaker. Tongues function in at least two common ways:

1. Private prayer/edification (praying mysteries to God)

2. Public message (requires interpretation)

"For he who speaks in a tongue does not speak to men but to God... however, in the spirit he speaks mysteries." (1 Corinthians 14:2, NKJV)

Godly fear guardrail

Tongues are not a mark of superiority. They must never become a reason for pride or division. And in public assembly, Scripture requires order and interpretation.

"If anyone speaks in a tongue, let there be two or at the most three... and let one interpret." (1 Corinthians 14:27, NKJV)

11) Interpretation of Tongues

What it is

Interpretation is not translation word-for-word necessarily; it is the Spirit giving the meaning of the public tongue, so the Church is edified.

"Therefore let him who speaks in a tongue pray that he may interpret." (1 Corinthians 14:13, NKJV)

What it does

- Makes the public tongue useful to the congregation

- Brings edification equivalent to prophecy in effect

- Maintains order and clarity in worship

Godly fear guardrail

Interpretation must not be fabricated. If the Spirit did not give it, do not force it. Better silence than presumption.

12) The Highest Order: Love Governs Gifts, and Holiness Guards Power

After listing gifts, Paul drops a divine safeguard: love.

"And now abide faith, hope, love, these three; but the greatest of these is love." (1 Corinthians 13:13, NKJV)

Why? Because gifts can operate through immature vessels, but love cannot thrive in a proud, unrepentant heart. Love exposes the true condition of the soul.

And holiness must guard power because gifts do not prove intimacy. Fruit proves abiding.

"By their fruits you will know them." (Matthew 7:16, NKJV)

So, this must provoke godly fear: do not chase gifts more than you chase Christ. Do not desire manifestations more than you desire sanctification. Do not celebrate power while neglecting purity.

13) How to Desire Gifts Biblically Without Becoming Strange or Proud

Paul commands desire—but with order:

"Pursue love, and desire spiritual gifts..." (1 Corinthians 14:1, NKJV)

A safe, biblical posture looks like this:

1. Pursue love first (character before charisma)

2. Stay anchored in Scripture (truth before experience)

3. Remain submitted (accountability protects gifting)

4. Keep repentance near (a clean vessel carries holy oil)

5. Seek edification (gifts are for the body, not ego)

6. Maintain order (God is not the author of confusion)
    "For God is not the author of confusion but of peace..." (1 Corinthians 14:33, NKJV)

14) A Final Warning That Restores Godly Fear: Do Not Mistake Manifestation for Maturity

Beloved, the Spirit can manifest through you, but you must still fear God and pursue holiness. Many have fallen because they thought gifting meant approval. Many assumed public power meant private purity. Many confused platform with presence.

This book is called UNQUENCHABLE GRACE OF GOD—and these gifts are truly grace. But grace is holy. Therefore:

- Do not merchandise the gifts.

- Do not perform with the gifts.

- Do not manipulate with the gifts.

- Do not boast in the gifts.

- Do not neglect holiness while using the gifts.

Let the gifts point people to Jesus, and let your life match your message.

Closing Scriptures for Meditation (NKJV)

- *"The manifestation of the Spirit is given... for the profit of all." (1 Corinthians 12:7)*

- *"...distributing to each one individually as He wills." (1 Corinthians 12:11)*

- *"Pursue love, and desire spiritual gifts..." (1 Corinthians 14:1)*

- *"Let all things be done decently and in order." (1 Corinthians 14:40)*

CHAPTER FIFTEEN: GRACE TO FIGHT AND STAND AGAINST THE WORKS OF DARKNESS — STRENGTH TO RESIST, DISCERN, AND OVERCOME WITHOUT COMPROMISE

Grace does not only save the believer from the penalty of sin. Grace also saves the believer from the power of sin—and equips the believer to stand against the kingdom of darkness.

Many believers have been taught to see grace as softness only—God's gentle kindness, God's patient mercy, God's forgiving heart. And that is true. But grace is also war-strength. Grace is the empowering presence of God that makes the believer unbendable in temptation, unmovable in trial, and unshakable in spiritual warfare.

Because the Christian life is not merely a journey—it is a battle. Not a battle for God to win (He has already won), but a battle for the believer to stand in what Christ has accomplished. And Scripture is clear: the believer is not called to negotiate with darkness, but to resist it.

"Be sober, be vigilant; because your adversary the devil walks about like a roaring lion, seeking whom he may devour. Resist him, steadfast in the faith..." (1 Peter 5:8–9, NKJV)

If the Spirit commands sobriety and resistance, then grace must supply the strength for it. God never commands what He does not empower. The command to stand assumes the supply of grace.

1) The First Battlefield: Grace to Fight Sin Within

Before we speak of demons and strongholds outside, we must begin where Scripture begins: the works of darkness first seek a foothold within the believer—through the flesh, lust, pride, bitterness, offense, and secret compromise.

Satan loves external noise, but his greatest victories are internal: a polluted conscience, a hardened heart, a double life, a prayerless soul, a mind addicted to impurity, a believer who calls sin "struggle" but refuses repentance.

So, grace to fight begins here: grace to deny the flesh.

"For the grace of God... teaching us that, denying ungodliness and worldly lusts, we should live soberly, righteously, and godly..." (Titus 2:11–12, NKJV)

Grace teaches denial. That denial is warfare. Every time a believer says "no" to lust, "no" to bitterness, "no" to pride, "no" to compromise— he is standing against darkness. Holiness is not passivity; holiness is resistance.

This is why the fear of the Lord is part of warfare. A believer who has lost godly fear has already opened the gate. But a believer who trembles at God's Word has built a wall of fire around his conscience.

2) Grace to Stand: The Mystery of Strength in Weakness

Standing does not always feel like victory. Sometimes standing feels like pressure, tears, endurance, and silent warfare. But standing is warfare.

"My grace is sufficient for you, for My strength is made perfect in weakness." (2 Corinthians 12:9, NKJV)

Grace does not always remove the storm; it makes the believer stable inside it. Grace does not always silence temptation; it provides power to resist it. Grace does not always take away the thorn; it supplies strength, so the thorn does not destroy the calling.

This is why the Christian who stands in weakness is not defeated—he is being strengthened by grace.

3) Grace to Discern: Seeing Darkness Clearly Without Becoming Paranoid

One of the most dangerous things in warfare is fighting the wrong enemy or misunderstanding the battlefield. The believer must discern what is flesh, what is demonic, what is circumstantial, and what is simply human weakness that needs discipline and repentance.

This is where the Spirit's gift and the Spirit's wisdom protect the believer. Discerning of spirits is not suspicion—it is spiritual sight. But even beyond the gift, grace teaches sobriety, so the believer does not become naive.

"Beloved, do not believe every spirit, but test the spirits…" (1 John 4:1, NKJV)

Grace gives discernment so the believer is not seduced by false doctrine, false prophets, counterfeit anointings, and "spiritual" experiences that are not of God. In the last days, deception will be bold. Therefore, grace to stand includes grace to test.

And godly fear is essential: because the believer who loves entertainment more than truth becomes easy prey.

4) Grace to Put On the Armor: Standing Is a Lifestyle, Not a Moment

Scripture does not say "put on the armor" once. It calls the believer to live armored.

"Put on the whole armor of God, that you may be able to stand against the wiles of the devil." (Ephesians 6:11, NKJV)

Notice: armor is about standing.

Grace fuels every piece of this armor:

- Truth (grace makes you love truth and hate lies)

- Righteousness (grace trains holiness, not hypocrisy)

- Gospel of peace (grace anchors you in reconciliation with God)

- Faith (grace strengthens trust, especially under attack)

- Salvation (grace keeps assurance pure and clean)

- Word of God (grace makes Scripture a sword, not a decoration)

- Prayer (grace fuels watchfulness and communion)

Without grace, armor becomes religious theory. With grace, armor becomes lived reality.

5) Grace to Resist the Devil: Spiritual Authority Without Compromise

Many want authority over demons but do not want authority over the flesh. Yet true authority flows through surrender.

"Therefore submit to God. Resist the devil and he will flee from you."
(James 4:7, NKJV)

Notice the order: submit, then resist.

Grace empowers submission. Grace empowers resistance. Grace teaches the believer to close doors: pornography, bitterness, occult exposure, unforgiveness, pride, lying, manipulation, drunkenness, compromise.

The devil flees not from religious noise, but from a submitted believer who stands in faith and holiness.

This is why grace is essential: because only grace can keep a believer submitted when pride wants control.

6) Grace to Fight in the Mind: Casting Down Strongholds

Many works of darkness operate through thoughts—condemnation, lustful imaginations, fear, accusation, hopelessness, suicidal whispering, and mental strongholds built through trauma and sin.

Spiritual warfare is often fought in the mind before it is seen in behavior.

"For the weapons of our warfare are not carnal but mighty in God for pulling down strongholds…" (2 Corinthians 10:4, NKJV)

Grace supplies these weapons:

- truth that breaks lies

- the blood of Jesus that silences condemnation

- the fear of the Lord that drives out secret sin

- the Word of God that renews the mind

- prayer that keeps the heart guarded

- praise that pushes back heaviness

A believer who neglects the mind will be defeated in private even while appearing strong in public. Grace teaches vigilance.

7) Grace to Fight Through Worship, Thanksgiving, and Purity

Darkness thrives in murmuring, complaining, bitterness, and impurity. But worship and thanksgiving are forms of warfare. They keep the heart aligned with heaven.

And Paul reveals a powerful connection:

"For all things are for your sakes, that grace, having spread through the many, may cause thanksgiving to abound to the glory of God." (2 Corinthians 4:15, NKJV)

Grace spreads → thanksgiving abounds → God is glorified.

That chain is warfare. Because thanksgiving kills entitlement. Worship breaks heaviness. Praise shifts the atmosphere. And God inhabits the praises of His people.

Grace fuels a worshiping, grateful heart—and darkness hates a heart that truly fears God and adores Christ.

8) Grace to Stand in Community: Isolation Is a Battlefield

The enemy loves isolated believers. Isolation breeds deception, lust, secret sin, discouragement, and false doctrine. Grace brings believers into light, fellowship, accountability, confession, and strengthening.

This is why Scripture says:

"Exhort one another daily… lest any of you be hardened through the deceitfulness of sin." (Hebrews 3:13, NKJV)

Sin deceives. Isolation empowers that deception. Grace breaks isolation by bringing the believer into the light.

If you want to stand against darkness, you must not fight alone.

9) A Deep Warning: Grace Is Not a Shield for Willful Sin

This must be said with trembling: the believer who uses grace to excuse sin is not "covered"—he is exposed. He is opening doors to darkness and then claiming protection while refusing repentance.

Hebrews warns against insulting the Spirit of grace (Hebrews 10:29, NKJV). That is warfare language. To insult grace is to weaken your own defenses.

So let godly fear return: repentance is not weakness; repentance is warfare. Confession is not defeat; confession is victory. Humility is not shame; humility is protection.

Grace empowers you to repent quickly and keep your garments clean.

10) Closing Exhortation: Stand by Grace, Walk in Light, and Do Not Give Place to Darkness

Beloved, grace is not a passive concept—it is a holy power. The grace that appeared in Christ is not only to bring salvation; it is to raise up a people who resist darkness and shine as lights in the world.

Do not flirt with what Christ died to destroy.

Do not call compromise "grace."

Do not silence conviction.

Do not tolerate what opens doors.

Do not neglect the Word.

Do not abandon prayer.

Do not isolate.

Instead, stand.

Stand in repentance.

Stand in truth.

Stand in holiness.

Stand in the Word.

Stand in prayer.

Stand in fellowship.

Stand in faith.

And when you feel weak, remember: the fight is not sustained by your strength, but by His grace.

"My grace is sufficient for you..." (2 Corinthians 12:9, NKJV)

Closing Scriptures for Meditation (NKJV)

- *"Be sober, be vigilant... Resist him, steadfast in the faith..." (1 Peter 5:8–9)*

- *"Put on the whole armor of God... to stand..." (Ephesians 6:11)*

- *"Submit to God. Resist the devil and he will flee..." (James 4:7)*

- *"The weapons of our warfare... mighty in God..." (2 Corinthians 10:4)*

- *"My grace is sufficient for you..." (2 Corinthians 12:9)*

CHAPTER SIXTEEN: EXCEEDING GRACE — GRACE THAT ABOUNDS BEYOND SIN, BEYOND WEAKNESS, AND BEYOND TRIALS, YET NEVER CANCELS GODLY FEAR

There is grace… and then there is exceeding grace.

Not grace as a small allowance. Not grace as a thin layer of mercy barely covering the believer. But grace that overflows—grace that abounds, multiplies, increases, spreads, and triumphs. Grace that reaches deeper than guilt, higher than accusation, stronger than temptation, and wider than failure.

Yet here is the holy balance we must keep: exceeding grace is not permission to sin more boldly. It is power to live more fully for Christ. Exceeding grace does not produce casualness; it produces worship. It does not cancel godly fear; it deepens reverence—because the more you see the abundance of mercy, the more you tremble at the thought of despising it.

Paul reveals one of the most breathtaking truths in the entire gospel:

"Moreover the law entered that the offense might abound. But where sin abounded, grace abounded much more." (Romans 5:20, NKJV)

Grace abounded much more. That is exceeding grace. It means grace is not merely equal to sin; grace surpasses sin. Grace is not merely a response; grace is a triumph. Grace is not merely healing; grace is resurrection.

1) Exceeding Grace Reveals the Heart of God — Mercy That Overcomes Our Worst

Many people can believe God forgives "small sins." But exceeding grace confronts a deeper disbelief: Can God forgive me after what I have done?

The answer of the gospel is yes—if you repent and come to Christ.

Exceeding grace is God's answer to the greatest stains. It is not minimizing sin—it is magnifying the power of the blood. It is not excusing rebellion—it is calling rebels home.

This is why the cross is the centerpiece of exceeding grace. Christ did not shed a little blood. He poured out His life. And the value of His sacrifice is not limited by the depth of your failure.

But do not misunderstand: grace is not cheap because it is abundant. It is abundant because the price was infinite.

2) Exceeding Grace Does Not Only Forgive Sin — It Breaks Sin's Dominion

Here is where we must go deeper: if grace abounds much more, it must do more than cancel guilt. It must also destroy bondage.

Paul immediately follows the "abounding grace" statement with a conclusion:

"For sin shall not have dominion over you, for you are not under law but under grace." (Romans 6:14, NKJV)

Exceeding grace is not a license to remain a slave; it is the power to become free. It does not merely say "you are forgiven" while leaving chains intact. It says, "you are forgiven" and then trains you, strengthens you, and empowers you to walk clean.

So, if someone claims exceeding grace but continues in willful sin without repentance, they are not living under grace—they are abusing the word grace while remaining under bondage.

Grace does not make sin safe. Grace makes holiness possible.

3) Exceeding Grace Is Seen Most Clearly in the Worst Failures Turned into Testimonies

Look at Scripture and see how exceeding grace works:

- David fell grievously, yet when broken, God restored him and used his tears to write psalms that still bring repentance to souls.

- Peter denied the Lord, yet Christ restored him and made him a pillar, not because Peter deserved it, but because grace restored what guilt would have destroyed.

- Paul persecuted the Church, yet God transformed him into an apostle and made his life a banner of mercy.

Paul said it plainly:

"But by the grace of God I am what I am…" (1 Corinthians 15:10, NKJV)

That is exceeding grace: not only erasing the past but transforming the future.

4) Exceeding Grace Spreads — It Multiplies Thanksgiving and Glory to God

Exceeding grace does not remain contained; it spreads into communities and multiplies worship.

"For all things are for your sakes, that grace, having spread through the many, may cause thanksgiving to abound to the glory of God." (2 Corinthians 4:15, NKJV)

Notice the chain:

- grace spreads

- thanksgiving abounds

- God is glorified

This is what exceeding grace produces: a people who are not proud, not entitled, not casual—but grateful, reverent, worshiping.

Where grace truly spreads, thanksgiving increases. And where thanksgiving increases, the spirit of entitlement dies. And where entitlement dies, holiness becomes precious again.

5) Exceeding Grace Produces Deeper Godly Fear — Because Mercy Is Not to Be Despised

Here is the necessary warning: abundant grace makes despising grace even more dangerous.

When God has been merciful, when He has forgiven much, when He has restored you repeatedly, and you still treat sin lightly—your heart is nearing a frightening place.

Paul warns:

"Do you despise the riches of His goodness, forbearance, and longsuffering...?" (Romans 2:4, NKJV)

The richer the goodness, the greater the guilt in despising it.

Exceeding grace should not make you bolder in sin; it should make you bolder in holiness. It should make you tremble at the thought of grieving the Spirit, insulting the blood, or trampling holy mercy.

This is true godly fear: not terror that God hates you, but reverence that loves Him too deeply to mock Him.

6) Exceeding Grace and the Danger of Presumption

Presumption is the counterfeit of faith. Presumption says, "God will forgive me anyway." Faith says, "I fear God; I will not sin against Him."

Presumption uses grace as a shield for rebellion. Faith uses grace as strength for obedience.

This is why Paul thundered:

"Shall we continue in sin that grace may abound? Certainly not!" (Romans 6:1–2, NKJV)

That question is the heartbeat of this chapter. Exceeding grace does not mean sin can increase safely. Exceeding grace means grace has come to end sin's reign and establish Christ's reign.

7) Exceeding Grace in Trials: Grace That Carries the Believer Beyond What Should Break Him

Exceeding grace is not only for failure—it is also for suffering.

Many believers have endured what should have destroyed them: persecution, betrayal, grief, sickness, loss, delay, warfare, loneliness. Yet they remained faithful. Not because they were naturally strong, but because grace carried them.

This is exceeding grace: the divine supply that keeps the believer from collapsing into bitterness, unbelief, or compromise.

"But may the God of all grace... after you have suffered a while, perfect, establish, strengthen, and settle you." (1 Peter 5:10, NKJV)

Grace that perfects. Grace that establishes. Grace that strengthens. Grace that settles. That is grace that exceeds the weight of the trial.

8) How to Live Under Exceeding Grace Without Abusing It

If you want exceeding grace to produce holiness, not hypocrisy, keep these holy guardrails:

1. Stay quick to repent — do not let sin linger.

2. Stay close to the cross — remember what grace cost.

3. Stay in the Word — grace does not contradict Scripture.

4. Stay in prayer — draw near to the throne of grace daily.

5. Stay accountable — darkness thrives in secrecy.

6. Stay thankful — thanksgiving protects you from entitlement.

7. Stay in godly fear — reverence guards mercy.

Closing Exhortation: Let Exceeding Grace Make You Tremble and Worship

Beloved, if grace has abounded toward you, do not treat it as common. If God has forgiven you, do not return to what He delivered you from. If

God has restored you, do not use restoration as a platform for compromise. If God has shown you mercy, let mercy produce holiness.

Exceeding grace is not a reason to sin.

Exceeding grace is the power to stop sin's dominion.

Exceeding grace is not a license.

Exceeding grace is fuel for worship, obedience, and perseverance.

Where sin abounded, grace abounded much more—so let Christ reign in you.

Closing Scriptures for Meditation (NKJV)

- *"Where sin abounded, grace abounded much more." (Romans 5:20)*

- *"For sin shall not have dominion over you... under grace." (Romans 6:14)*

- *"Grace... having spread... thanksgiving to abound..." (2 Corinthians 4:15)*

- *"Do you despise the riches of His goodness...?" (Romans 2:4)*

- *"May the God of all grace... perfect, establish, strengthen, and settle you." (1 Peter 5:10)*

CHAPTER SEVENTEEN: ELECTION BY GRACE — MERCY THAT REMOVES BOASTING, CALLS FOR HUMILITY, AND WARNS AGAINST UNBELIEF

There are few subjects that humble the soul like election—when it is understood biblically.

Election is not given so the believer can feel superior. Election is not a trophy for religious pride. Election is not permission to become careless. Election is meant to do the opposite: to destroy boasting, exalt mercy, and produce trembling gratitude. It is meant to make a believer fall on his face and say, "Lord, if You had not chosen to show mercy, I would have been lost forever."

And Scripture anchors election in one place—grace:

"Even so then, at this present time there is a remnant according to the election of grace. And if by grace, then it is no longer of works; otherwise grace is no longer grace." (Romans 11:5–6, NKJV)

Paul does not say "election of works." He says election of grace. That means election is rooted in God's mercy—not man's merit. It is rooted in God's purpose—not human performance. It is rooted in God's initiative—not man's self-salvation.

Yet this same chapter of Romans is filled with warnings to keep the believer in godly fear—warnings against pride, unbelief, and being cut off. So, this chapter must be handled with both wonder and trembling.

1) What Is Election? — God's Merciful Choosing, Not Man's Self-Selection

Election, in its simplest biblical sense, means God chooses. He calls. He sets apart. He appoints. He draws. He saves.

Salvation is not man finding God first; it is God finding man. It is the Shepherd seeking the lost sheep. It is the Father drawing the prodigal home. It is Christ calling the dead out of the grave.

We did not initiate salvation—God did.

This is why election magnifies grace: because it makes salvation entirely dependent on God's mercy. If salvation began with man, man could boast. But since salvation begins with God, all glory belongs to Him.

"Therefore it is not of him who wills, nor of him who runs, but of God who shows mercy." (Romans 9:16, NKJV)

Election humbles the will. It humbles human effort. It humbles pride.

2) "Election of Grace" — The Death of Boasting

Romans 11:5–6 is a sword against pride:

"And if by grace, then it is no longer of works; otherwise grace is no longer grace." (Romans 11:6, NKJV)

This means you cannot mix election with self-righteousness. You cannot say, "God chose me because I was better." You cannot say, "God chose me because I deserved it." You cannot say, "God chose me because I outperformed others."

Election is not God rewarding the righteous; it is God saving the undeserving.

So, if you utterly understand election, you cannot remain proud. Election produces humility. It makes the believer grateful, not arrogant. It makes the believer gentle, not harsh—because he knows his salvation is mercy.

3) The Purpose of Election: A Remnant Who Belongs to God

Paul says:

"...there is a remnant according to the election of grace." (Romans 11:5, NKJV)

A remnant is a people preserved by God—kept from total corruption, kept through judgment, kept for His purposes. Throughout Scripture, God has always kept a remnant: those who remain faithful when many fall away.

Election, then, is not merely about "who gets in." It is about God preserving a people for Himself—a people who will bear His name, carry His truth, and live as His testimony in the earth.

This reveals something crucial: election is not meant to produce spiritual laziness; it is meant to produce faithfulness. The remnant is not careless. The remnant fears God. The remnant endures.

4) A Deep Warning: Election Does Not Justify Pride—Pride Leads to Being Cut Off

Romans 11 is not only mercy; it is also warning. Paul specifically warns Gentile believers not to become arrogant toward Israel, and not to presume upon grace.

"Do not be haughty, but fear." (Romans 11:20, NKJV)

Those words should shake every heart: "…but fear."

And Paul continues:

"For if God did not spare the natural branches, He may not spare you either. Therefore consider the goodness and severity of God…" (Romans 11:21–22, NKJV)

This is not written to unbelievers. It is written as a warning to those who stand by faith. It reveals the balance of the gospel:

- Goodness: mercy, grace, salvation, kindness

- Severity: judgment against unbelief, cutting off, accountability

And the conclusion is sobering:

"…toward you, goodness, if you continue in His goodness. Otherwise you also will be cut off." (Romans 11:22, NKJV)

This is why my book's theme—godly fear and not taking grace for granted—fits perfectly here. Election of grace does not remove the call to continue in faith; it intensifies it.

5) Election and Responsibility: Grace Does Not Cancel Perseverance

Here is where many err: they treat election as if it makes obedience optional and perseverance unnecessary. But Scripture does not speak like that. Scripture says:

- We are saved by grace through faith.

- We must continue in faith.

- We must abide in Christ.

- We must not harden our hearts.

- We must not drift into unbelief.

Election magnifies grace, but it does not remove the reality of warnings. The warnings are one of the means by which God keeps the remnant sober and watchful.

So, election should not make you careless. It should make you vigilant.

"Beware, brethren, lest there be in any of you an evil heart of unbelief..." (Hebrews 3:12, NKJV)

If unbelief is possible to warn against, then continuing in faith is a serious matter. Grace is unquenchable, but the human heart must not be hardened.

6) The True Evidence of Election: A Life Marked by Humility, Faith, and Holiness

A person who truly understands "election by grace" will display certain fruits:

- humility (no boasting, no superiority)

- gratitude (thanksgiving abounds)

- repentance (a tender conscience)

- faith (continuing, abiding, persevering)

- holiness (grace trains them to deny ungodliness)

- love (they desire others to be saved, not judged)

Election that produces pride is not biblical understanding; it is deception.

Because election by grace always points the heart to the cross.

7) A Call to the Reader: Let Election Produce Fear of God, Not Pride of Doctrine

Beloved, if God has shown you mercy, the only right response is surrender. If God has chosen to reveal Christ to you, the only safe response is to walk in reverence.

Do not turn election into a theological weapon.

Do not turn election into a reason to judge others.

Do not turn election into spiritual laziness.

Do not turn election into "once safe, always safe no matter how I live."

Instead, let election lead you to worship and trembling:

- "Lord, thank You for mercy."

- "Lord, keep me from pride."

- "Lord, keep me from unbelief."

- "Lord, establish me by Your grace."

- "Lord, make me part of Your faithful remnant."

Because Romans 11 does not end with arrogance—it ends with awe:

"Oh, the depth of the riches both of the wisdom and knowledge of God!" (Romans 11:33, NKJV)

That is where election should bring you: to worship.

Closing Scriptures for Meditation (NKJV)

- *"...a remnant according to the election of grace." (Romans 11:5)*

- *"And if by grace, then it is no longer of works..." (Romans 11:6)*

- *"Do not be haughty, but fear." (Romans 11:20)*

- *"...goodness and severity of God..." (Romans 11:22)*

CHAPTER EIGHTEEN: FINDING GRACE IN THE SIGHT OF GOD — THE SECRET OF A LIFE GOD FAVORS, AND THE FEAR THAT KEEPS GRACE PRECIOUS

(Going Deeper: "Found Grace" Is Not Random—It Is God's Mercy Meeting a Humble Heart)

There is a phrase in Scripture that should stop every believer in reverence:

"Found grace…"

"Found favor…"

"In the sight of the LORD…"

It appears in moments of judgment, in moments of transition, in moments where God is separating the pure from the corrupt, the obedient from the rebellious, the humble from the proud. This phrase is not casual. It carries weight. It reveals something sacred: God looks. God sees. God evaluates. God weighs hearts. And in the midst of a crooked world, He still grants grace.

But we must go deeper: "finding grace" is not God playing favorites like a man. It is not random luck. It is not arbitrary selection. It is the mercy of God meeting a heart that fears Him, walks with Him, and refuses the spirit of the age.

And if a believer understands this phrase rightly, it will provoke godly fear—not fear that God is unfair, but fear that God is holy, and that His favor must never be treated lightly.

1) "In the Eyes of the LORD" — Grace Is Found Before God's Face, Not Before Men

When Scripture says someone found grace "in the eyes of the LORD," it reveals that grace is not primarily about public approval. It is about divine sight.

Men may applaud you and heaven may disapprove.

Men may reject you and heaven may favor you.

Men may not understand your obedience, but God sees.

This is why finding grace begins with living before God, not before people. It is the death of performance Christianity. It is walking in truth in the secret place, where no one is watching but the One who matters most.

2) Noah: Grace Found in a Generation Under Judgment

The first major "found grace" statement is terrifying in its context:

"But Noah found grace in the eyes of the LORD." (Genesis 6:8, NKJV)

Read it slowly. Noah found grace while judgment was forming. Noah found grace while the earth was filled with violence and corruption. Noah found grace while humanity was ripening for destruction.

This reveals a crucial truth: grace is not only God's kindness; grace is also God's separating mercy. Grace marks a man out for preservation when others are swept away.

And what did Noah do?

"Noah was a just man, perfect in his generations. Noah walked with God." (Genesis 6:9, NKJV)

"Perfect" here does not mean sinless. It means integrity, whole-heartedness—undivided devotion. Noah was not double-minded. He did not flirt with corruption. He did not compromise with the culture. He walked with God.

Here is the deeper revelation: Noah's life was aligned with the grace he found. Grace did not make him careless; grace made him faithful. Grace did not excuse him from obedience; grace empowered him to obey.

Noah's grace was not mere forgiveness—it was favor that produced obedience strong enough to build an ark for a world that mocked him.

So, the question becomes personal:

If God is looking upon this generation, what does He see in me?

3) Moses: Grace Found That Led to Intimacy and the Knowledge of God's Ways

Moses also spoke this phrase with trembling desire:

"Now therefore, I pray, if I have found grace in Your sight, show me now Your way, that I may know You..." (Exodus 33:13, NKJV)

Notice what Moses asks. He does not ask first for gifts, fame, or comfort. He asks: "Show me Your way, that I may know You."

This is deeper than blessing. This is hunger for intimacy.

Here is the revelation: finding grace in God's sight creates desire to know God, not merely to use God. Grace leads to relationship. Grace awakens longing for God's presence.

And Moses presses further:

"And He said, 'My Presence will go with you, and I will give you rest.'"
(Exodus 33:14, NKJV)

Grace led Moses into the presence of God. Grace produced communion. Grace did not merely grant a miracle—it granted nearness.

But Moses did not treat it casually. He trembled. He pleaded. He valued God's presence above the journey itself:

"If Your Presence does not go with us, do not bring us up from here."
(Exodus 33:15, NKJV)

That is godly fear: valuing God above outcomes, valuing presence above success, valuing holiness above advancement.

4) Finding Grace and Godly Fear: Grace Is Given, But Grace Is Also Guarded

Let's go deeper: Scripture shows that grace is found—and grace can also be fallen short of.

"Looking carefully lest anyone fall short of the grace of God..."
(Hebrews 12:15, NKJV)

This means grace is not a casual possession. A believer must walk carefully. Not in anxious torment, but in holy sobriety—guarding the heart from bitterness, unbelief, and sin that hardens.

Noah found grace and walked with God.

Moses found grace and pursued God's presence.

Grace was not only received; grace was honored.

This is the dividing line between true believers and careless Christians: true believers honor grace with fear of God.

5) The Pattern of "Finding Grace": What God Honors

While grace is never earned like wages, Scripture reveals patterns—postures God honors. These are not merits to boast in; they are humble alignments with God.

A) Humility

"God resists the proud, but gives grace to the humble." (James 4:6, NKJV)

This is direct. Pride blocks grace. Humility receives grace. A proud believer may know Bible verses, but he will be spiritually dry. A humble believer may feel weak, but he will be supplied.

B) Obedience

Noah's obedience was the proof of his faith.

Moses' obedience was the pathway to intimacy.

Grace never makes obedience optional. It makes obedience possible.

C) Separation from Corruption

Noah was "perfect in his generations." He refused the spirit of the age. In end-time language, he refused the mark of cultural corruption.

A believer who wants grace but loves the world is double-minded—and double-mindedness leads to instability.

D) Hunger for God's Presence

Moses shows us the heart that finds grace: "that I may know You." Grace is not merely protection; it is invitation into communion.

6) Grace in the Sight of God Versus Favor in the Sight of Men

Many believers chase doors, networks, applause, and platform. But Scripture calls us to something higher: to live for God's eyes.

Grace in God's sight may cost you acceptance with men. Noah looked foolish. Moses was criticized. Jesus was rejected. Yet heaven's favor rested upon them.

This is where the fear of the Lord becomes liberation: when you fear God, you are free from fearing man.

And this also protects the believer from using grace to become proud. If your heart is living for God's approval, you cannot boast—because you know God sees the secret.

7) A Deep Warning: Grace Can Be Received and Still Be Despised

This must be said plainly: some receive grace outwardly—through exposure to truth, through blessings, through deliverance—and still despise it inwardly by refusing repentance.

"Or do you despise the riches of His goodness… not knowing that the goodness of God leads you to repentance?" (Romans 2:4, NKJV)

Despising grace is not always loud. It can look like delay in repentance. It can look like tolerated sin. It can look like bitterness that is kept. It can look like prayerlessness. It can look like resisting conviction repeatedly.

So, this chapter calls the believer to fear God: if you have found grace, honor it. Guard it. Do not treat it as common.

8) A Call to the Reader: How Do You "Find Grace" Today?

Beloved, if you desire to find grace in the sight of God—not as a boast, but as a holy longing—then let Scripture lead you into a posture:

1. Humble yourself — repent of pride and self-rule.

2. Walk in the light — refuse secret compromise.

3. Obey promptly — delayed obedience is often disguised rebellion.

4. Treasure God's presence — prefer Him above answers.

5. Stay tender — forgive quickly; do not allow roots of bitterness.

6. Fear God — not as terror, but as reverent love that hates sin.

7. Seek to know His ways — not merely His benefits.

This is not earning grace. This is honoring grace.

Because grace is not merely something God gives you—it is also a realm you must walk in with reverence.

Closing Exhortation: Let Grace Make You Walk with God

Noah found grace and walked with God.

Moses found grace and pursued God's presence.

And the Church is called to the same: to live before God's eyes, to fear Him, to honor His mercy, and to walk in holiness.

If you have found grace, do not waste it.

If you have found mercy, do not despise it.

If God has favored you, do not flirt with sin.

If His eyes have looked upon you, then let your heart look upon Him.

May the Lord make you a Noah in this generation—walking with God.

May the Lord make you a Moses in this hour—hungry for His presence.

And may your life prove that grace is not a small thing, but a holy treasure.

Closing Scriptures for Meditation (NKJV)

- *"But Noah found grace in the eyes of the LORD." (Genesis 6:8)*

- *"Noah... walked with God." (Genesis 6:9)*

- *"If I have found grace in Your sight... show me now Your way, that I may know You..." (Exodus 33:13)*

- *"Looking carefully lest anyone fall short of the grace of God..." (Hebrews 12:15)*

- *"God resists the proud but gives grace to the humble." (James 4:6)*

CHAPTER NINETEEN: THE WORD OF HIS GRACE — THE LIVING MESSAGE THAT BUILDS THE BELIEVER, GUARDS THE SOUL, AND LEAVES NO ROOM FOR CASUAL CHRISTIANITY

Grace is not only something God feels toward you.

Grace is not only something God gives to you.

Grace is also something God speaks to you.

In Scripture, grace has a voice. Grace comes with a message. Grace is carried through proclamation. Grace enters the heart through truth. And if a believer neglects the Word, he will eventually weaken in grace—because the Word is one of the primary channels through which grace strengthens, corrects, and establishes the soul.

This is why the apostles did not treat preaching as optional. They understood that when the Word of God is released, grace is released. When truth is spoken, grace persuades. When Scripture is received, grace trains. When the Word is neglected, the heart drifts.

The Bible even gives the gospel a sacred name:

"...speaking boldly in the Lord, who was bearing witness to the word of His grace..." (Acts 14:3, NKJV)

And again, as Paul prepared to depart from the elders he loved, he entrusted them to one thing above all:

"So now, brethren, I commend you to God and to the word of His grace, which is able to build you up and give you an inheritance among all those who are sanctified." (Acts 20:32, NKJV)

This chapter is about that phrase: the word of His grace—and why godly fear must guard our relationship with Scripture.

1) "The Word of His Grace" — Grace Comes Through Divine Communication

God could have chosen to save and sanctify people through mysteries only, private feelings only, visions only. But He chose something profoundly stable: His Word.

Grace is not vague. Grace is not shapeless. Grace is defined by the Word. This is why the devil always attacks Scripture: if he can distort the Word, he can distort grace; and if he can distort grace, he can destroy holiness while people still think they are safe.

The "word of His grace" is the gospel message centered in Christ— His incarnation, death, resurrection, lordship, and the call to repent and believe. It is also the entire counsel of God that builds the believer into maturity.

So, grace is not merely an emotion from heaven; it is the truth of God entering the mind and heart.

2) The Word of Grace Is Able to "Build You Up" — Grace Strengthens Through Scripture

Paul says the word of His grace is able to build you up. That is spiritual construction language. It means the Word strengthens structure: faith, doctrine, endurance, discernment, holiness, and stability.

Many believers fall into cycles because they live on feelings instead of the Word. They are moved by inspiration but not anchored by truth. They are excited in worship, but weak in temptation. They love sermons, but they do not eat Scripture daily.

But the Word builds. It renews the mind. It exposes lies. It strengthens conscience. It trains the soul to resist sin.

And because of that, the Word is one of the greatest expressions of sustaining grace God gives a believer.

If you want to stand strong in grace, you must be built by the Word.

3) The Word of Grace "Gives an Inheritance" — The Word Keeps You on the Path of Sanctification

Paul continues:

"...and give you an inheritance among all those who are sanctified."
(Acts 20:32, NKJV)

Notice: inheritance is connected to sanctification. The Word of grace is able to bring you into inheritance among those who are sanctified—those being set apart, purified, trained, transformed.

This is why the Word cannot be separated from holiness. Any "grace" message that removes sanctification is not the word of His grace. The word of His grace builds and sanctifies. It does not entertain sin. It does not flatter the flesh. It does not soothe rebellion. It calls the believer to purity and perseverance.

Grace that does not sanctify is not biblical grace—it is a counterfeit comfort.

4) Acts 14:3 — When the Word of Grace Is Spoken, God Bears Witness

Acts 14:3 shows a divine partnership: the apostles spoke, and God bore witness.

This reveals a deep truth: when the Word of grace is proclaimed boldly and faithfully, God confirms it—through conviction, through changed hearts, through healing, through deliverance, through spiritual awakening.

But this also reveals the seriousness of preaching: if the Word is twisted, the people are damaged. False grace creates false assurance. False grace produces lawlessness. False grace lulls souls to sleep while hell opens its mouth.

Therefore, the preacher and the hearer must both fear God:

- The preacher must fear God to preach the truth.

- The hearer must fear God to receive the truth.

5) The Most Dangerous Thing: Neglecting the Word While Claiming Grace

The writer of Hebrews gives a sobering warning:

"...how shall we escape if we neglect so great a salvation...?"
(Hebrews 2:3, NKJV)

Neglect is dangerous because it is quiet. Neglect is not dramatic rebellion; it is slow drift. It is skipping prayer. Skipping Scripture. Silencing conviction. Tolerating compromise. Feeding the flesh. Becoming entertained by the world. Remaining religious—but not alive.

And this is exactly how many "fall short of the grace of God" (Hebrews 12:15)—not through a sudden denial, but through gradual neglect.

The Word of His grace is one of God's chief tools to prevent neglect. The Word keeps you awake. The Word keeps you sober. The Word keeps your conscience sharp. The Word keeps the fear of God alive.

When the Word is neglected, grace is taken for granted.

6) The Word of Grace Exposes False Grace

False grace is one of the greatest end-time deceptions. It sounds like freedom but produces bondage. It sounds like love but removes holiness. It sounds like safety but removes godly fear.

The antidote is the Word.

The Word of grace teaches that grace trains us to deny ungodliness (Titus 2:11–12).

The Word of grace warns against receiving grace in vain (2 Corinthians 6:1).

The Word of grace warns against falling short (Hebrews 12:15).

The Word of grace warns against insulting the Spirit of grace (Hebrews 10:29).

So, the Word does not only comfort; it confronts. The Word does not only promise; it warns. The Word does not only heal; it cuts away deception.

That is grace.

7) A Deep Call to Godly Fear: Treat Scripture as Holy Bread, Not Background Noise

Beloved, if grace is unquenchable, one of the ways we honor it is by honoring the Word that carries it.

Do not treat Scripture like an accessory.

Do not treat preaching like entertainment.

Do not treat correction like condemnation.

Do not treat conviction like negativity.

The Word of His grace is life. It is bread. It is fire. It is a sword. It is a lamp. It is a mirror. It is the voice of God calling you to life.

A believer who loves grace, but neglects Scripture will eventually redefine grace into something the Bible does not teach.

So, fear God enough to stay in His Word.

8) Practical Ways to Live Under "The Word of His Grace"

To be built by the Word of His grace:

1. Read daily — not for information only, but communion and obedience.

2. Receive correction — let the Word confront your sin, not just comfort your emotions.

3. Memorize key passages — store grace-truth in your heart for warfare.

4. Test everything — measure teachings, dreams, and prophecies by Scripture.

5. Obey quickly — delayed obedience hardens the heart.

6. Stay teachable — pride blocks grace; humility receives grace.

7. Return often — the Word is not a one-time visit; it is daily bread.

Closing Exhortation: If You Want to Stand in Grace, Stand Under the Word

Paul did not commend the elders to programs, charisma, or popularity. He commended them to God and to the word of His grace—because that Word builds, sanctifies, and brings believers into inheritance.

If you want to keep the fear of God alive, stay in the Word.

If you want to resist deception, stay in the Word.

If you want to grow in grace, stay in the Word.

If you want to endure to the end, stay in the Word.

Because the Word of His grace is still building the remnant.

Closing Scriptures for Meditation (NKJV)

- *"...the word of His grace, which is able to build you up..." (Acts 20:32)*

- *"...bearing witness to the word of His grace..." (Acts 14:3)*

- *"...how shall we escape if we neglect so great a salvation...?" (Hebrews 2:3)*

- *"Looking carefully lest anyone fall short of the grace of God..." (Hebrews 12:15)*

CHAPTER TWENTY: EXPOSITION: 1 PETER 5:10 (NKJV)

"But may the God of all grace, who called us to His eternal glory by Christ Jesus, after you have suffered a while, perfect, establish, strengthen, and settle you."

The Divine Progression in 1 Peter 5:10

Here is the flow of the Spirit's word:

1. Perfect — God repairs and matures what suffering exposed

2. Establish — God roots you, so you stop drifting

3. Strengthen — God infuses inner power to endure and obey

4. Settle — God makes you steady, calm, and unshakable

This is what "the God of all grace" does to believers who endure trials with faith.

Perfected by Grace — The God of All Grace Restoring What Is Lacking After You Have Suffered a While

"But may the God of all grace, who called us to His eternal glory by Christ Jesus, after you have suffered a while, perfect..." (1 Peter 5:10, NKJV)

There are seasons where God does not change the storm—He changes the vessel. There are moments when the Lord does not remove the pressure—He uses the pressure to reveal what is still incomplete in us. Not to shame us. Not to crush us. But to perfect us by grace.

This word "perfect" in 1 Peter 5:10 is not the modern idea of flawlessness, as though God is demanding you never stumble. It carries the sense of restoring, mending, repairing, and bringing to maturity—like a skilled craftsman setting what has been out of place, healing what was fractured, and completing what was lacking.

Grace does not merely forgive the believer. Grace repairs the believer.

1) Perfecting Grace Begins Where Suffering Exposes the Truth

Suffering has a way of uncovering what comfort hides. When life is smooth, a believer may assume he is strong. But when pressure comes, the heart is revealed: impatience, fear, pride, unbelief, hidden cravings, bitterness, self-reliance, spiritual laziness, secret compromise.

Yet the God of all grace does not expose to humiliate—He exposes to heal.

"Search me, O God, and know my heart; try me, and know my anxieties; and see if there is any wicked way in me..." (Psalm 139:23–24, NKJV)

Perfecting grace is God answering that prayer in real time. It is God saying, "I will not let you carry hidden fractures into your next season."

2) Perfecting Grace Is God Setting the Inner Man in Order

Some believers want grace to only comfort them. But grace also corrects. Grace trains. Grace confronts. Grace sets the inner man back into alignment with heaven.

"For the grace of God... has appeared... teaching us that, denying ungodliness and worldly lusts, we should live soberly..." (Titus 2:11–12, NKJV)

When grace perfects you, it does not only remove guilt—it removes deception. It teaches you to call sin what God calls it. It teaches you to stop making peace with what Christ died to destroy. It teaches you to stop living in spiritual half-measures.

Perfecting grace is grace that refuses to leave you immature.

3) Perfecting Grace Is How God Restores a Fallen Believer Without Destroying Him

There are believers who stumble grievously and assume God is finished with them. But perfecting grace restores. It does not excuse sin—but it heals the repentant.

"If we confess our sins, He is faithful and just to forgive us our sins and to cleanse us from all unrighteousness." (1 John 1:9, NKJV)

Notice: forgive and cleanse. Perfecting grace cleanses the roots. It goes deeper than the act. It deals with the appetite, the motive, the hidden door, the secrecy, the pride that resisted correction.

Grace does not merely say, "You are forgiven." It says, "Come—let Me make you whole."

4) Perfecting Grace Produces a Mature Conscience

An immature believer argues with conviction. A perfected believer treasures conviction.

Perfecting grace makes the conscience tender again. It restores spiritual sensitivity. It makes you fear grieving the Spirit. It makes you quick to repent. It makes you allergic to compromise.

"Looking carefully lest anyone fall short of the grace of God; lest any root of bitterness springing up cause trouble..." (Hebrews 12:15, NKJV)

Bitterness is often a fracture that suffering exposes. Perfecting grace uproots it—if the believer yields.

5) The Cooperation of the Vessel: Perfecting Grace Is Resisted by Pride

Perfecting grace requires humility. The proud believer refuses correction and remains broken in places he pretends are whole.

"God resists the proud, but gives grace to the humble." (James 4:6, NKJV)

If you want to be perfected by grace, you must allow God to name what is wrong. You must stop defending what He is confronting. You must stop excusing what He is exposing. This is where godly fear becomes protection: it keeps the heart soft.

6) Closing Exhortation: Let the God of All Grace Finish His Work

Beloved, do not rush past the perfecting of the Lord. Do not demand the next chapter while resisting the inner repair. Many want promotion with fractures still inside—then the weight of the next season breaks them.

So, yield.

Let grace mend you.

Let grace mature you.

Let grace cleanse you.

Let grace correct you.

Let grace restore your inner structure until Christ is formed in you.

"For He who has begun a good work in you will complete it…"
(Philippians 1:6, NKJV)

Closing Scriptures for Meditation (NKJV)

- *(1 Peter 5:10)*

- *(Titus 2:11–12)*

- *(1 John 1:9)*

- *(Hebrews 12:15)*

- *(James 4:6)*

Established by Grace — Strengthened in the Inner Man, Rooted in Truth, and Kept from Drifting

There is a difference between a believer who is saved and a believer who is established.

Many are truly born again, yet they remain unstable—tossed by emotions, shaken by trials, easily offended, easily deceived, easily discouraged, easily pulled back into old patterns. They love God, yet they are not grounded. They hear truth, yet they still drift. They desire holiness, yet they are inconsistent.

This is why the Scripture speaks not only of grace that saves, but grace that establishes—grace that strengthens the heart, roots the soul, and makes the believer firm.

Grace is not only the doorway into the Christian life. Grace is also the foundation that keeps the house from collapsing.

The Holy Spirit makes this clear:

"But may the God of all grace… after you have suffered a while, perfect, establish, strengthen, and settle you." (1 Peter 5:10, NKJV)

This is grace establishing.

1) To Be "Established" Means to Be Made Firm, Stable, and Unmovable

Established believers are not sinless, but they are anchored. They do not live on spiritual hype. They do not depend on moods. They do not panic every time the wind of life blows. They stand in truth.

To be established means:

- your doctrine is rooted

- your conscience is tender

- your obedience is consistent

- your faith endures pressure

- your mind is renewed

- your heart is strengthened

- your love is growing

- your repentance is quick

- your walk is steady

And the source is not willpower. The source is grace.

2) The God of All Grace Establishes Through Process: "After You Have Suffered a While"

Peter ties establishment to suffering:

"... after you have suffered a while..." (1 Peter 5:10, NKJV)

Here is a deep truth: many believers want stability without the process that produces stability. But God often establishes through pressure. He uses trials to deepen roots. He uses delay to train endurance. He uses warfare to sharpen discernment. He uses weakness to teach dependence.

A tree that grows in calm conditions may look tall, but it breaks easily in storms. A tree that grows in wind develops strong roots. Likewise, suffering—under grace—does not destroy the believer; it establishes the believer.

But only if the believer yields.

If you resist grace in suffering, you become bitter.

If you receive grace in suffering, you become established.

3) Grace Establishes by Strengthening the Heart, Not Only Changing Circumstances

Many believers measure God's help by outward change. But God's deepest work is inward.

Grace establishes by strengthening:

- the will to obey

- the conscience to remain clean

- the mind to reject lies

- the heart to resist bitterness

- the spirit to endure pressure

- the soul to remain in peace

This is why grace is sufficient: because grace does not only address what is happening to you; it addresses what is happening in you.

4) Established by Grace Means Anchored in "The Word of His Grace"

Paul already gave the pathway:

"...the word of His grace, which is able to build you up..." (Acts 20:32, NKJV)

Grace establishes through the Word. If a believer wants stability but neglects Scripture, he is trying to stand without foundation. The Word builds doctrine, convicts sin, renews the mind, and produces spiritual maturity.

This is why many are unstable: they love sermons but do not live in Scripture. They consume inspiration but lack formation.

The Word of grace establishes because it does two things at once:

- it comforts the repentant

- it confronts the careless

Both are necessary for maturity.

5) Grace Establishes by Protecting Against False Doctrine and False "Grace"

One of the greatest reasons believers must be established is because deception is increasing. There is a grace message that is true—and there is a grace message that is counterfeit.

True grace trains holiness (Titus 2:11–12).

False grace excuses sin (Jude 1:4).

True grace produces repentance.

False grace produces presumption.

So, to be established by grace is to be established in the true gospel—so you are not tossed by every new teaching, trend, or personality-driven doctrine.

This is why godly fear matters: a believer who fears God will test what he hears. A believer who loves comfort more than truth will swallow deception easily.

6) Grace Establishes Through Humility: Pride Creates Instability

The proud believer is unstable because pride refuses correction. Pride resists conviction. Pride justifies itself. Pride hides sin. Pride blames others. Pride cannot be taught.

But grace flows to the humble:

"God resists the proud, but gives grace to the humble." (James 4:6, NKJV)

So, establishment requires humility—not as an optional virtue, but as a spiritual necessity. God establishes those who stay low enough to be corrected.

A humble believer may be weak, but he is teachable—therefore he grows.

A proud believer may look strong, but he is uncorrectable—therefore he drifts.

Grace establishes the humble.

7) Grace Establishes Through Continual Repentance and a Clean Conscience

Unconfessed sin creates spiritual instability. It weakens faith, darkens discernment, and drains confidence before God.

Grace establishes by keeping repentance near.

Not repentance as condemnation—but repentance as cleansing, restoring, re-aligning the heart.

A believer who repents quickly stays established.

A believer who delays repentance becomes unstable.

This is why fear of God is protection: it makes you turn quickly.

8) The Fear of the Lord Is Part of Being Established

To be established by grace is not to be careless. It is to be stable in holy reverence.

Romans 11 already warned:

"Do not be haughty, but fear." (Romans 11:20, NKJV)

The established believer has learned the balance:

- confidence in God's mercy

- fear of drifting into sin

- assurance in Christ

- hatred for compromise

- peace in trials

- vigilance in temptation

This is the mature posture of grace: secure, but sober.

9) Signs You Are Becoming Established by Grace

Here are marks that grace is establishing you:

- You are less moved by people's opinions.

- You return to prayer faster when you drift.

- You repent quickly when convicted.

- You hunger for Scripture more than entertainment.

- You endure trials without bitterness.

- You resist sin sooner, not later.

- You test doctrine rather than absorbing everything.

- You stay faithful in secret, not only in public.

- You are increasingly steady, not increasingly dramatic.

This is not self-improvement. This is grace building a foundation.

Closing Exhortation: Let Grace Establish You Until You Are Unshakable

Beloved, God did not save you to remain unstable. He saved you to become steadfast. He saved you to endure. He saved you to stand. And the grace that saved you is also able to establish you.

So, draw near to the throne.

Stay under the Word of His grace.

Keep your conscience clean.

Walk in humility.

Fear God.

Resist darkness.

Endure with patience.

And may the God of all grace perfect, establish, strengthen, and settle you—so your life becomes a pillar of testimony in this generation.

Closing Scriptures for Meditation (NKJV)

- *"May the God of all grace... perfect, establish, strengthen, and settle you." (1 Peter 5:10)*

- *"...the word of His grace, which is able to build you up..." (Acts 20:32)*

- *"God resists the proud, but gives grace to the humble." (James 4:6)*

- *"Do not be haughty, but fear." (Romans 11:20)*

Strengthened by Grace — Divine Power in the Inner Man to Endure, Obey, Resist, and Stand

"But may the God of all grace... after you have suffered a while... strengthen..." (1 Peter 5:10, NKJV)

The Christian life is not sustained by inspiration alone. It is sustained by strength—and that strength is not natural. It is grace.

Many believers are sincere but weak. They love God, yet temptation overwhelms them. They want holiness, yet pressure bends them. They begin well, yet they grow weary and drift. What they need is not a new personality. What they need is strengthened grace.

Strengthened grace is the supply of God that makes the believer firm under pressure and faithful in obedience.

1) Strengthening Grace Is Not Hype—It Is Holy Stamina

Spiritual strength is not loudness. It is endurance. It is the ability to keep obeying when feelings fade. It is the ability to remain pure when lust knocks. It is the ability to stand in truth when compromise is celebrated.

"My grace is sufficient for you, for My strength is made perfect in weakness." (2 Corinthians 12:9, NKJV)

God's strength appears most clearly when your strength runs out. That is why grace strengthens—so the glory belongs to Christ, not to human willpower.

2) Strengthening Grace Powers Obedience

Grace does not lower God's standard; it empowers the believer to walk in it.

"But by the grace of God I am what I am... I labored... yet not I, but the grace of God which was with me." (1 Corinthians 15:10, NKJV)

Grace "with me." That is strengthening grace—present help, living supply, divine enabling. This is why a believer cannot say, "I had no power to obey." Not if he is drawing near to the throne and walking in the Spirit.

3) Strengthening Grace Is How God Keeps You in Warfare

The command to stand assumes grace to stand.

"Be sober, be vigilant... Resist him, steadfast in the faith..." (1 Peter 5:8–9, NKJV)

Grace strengthens the believer to resist, not negotiate. It strengthens the believer to shut doors: secret sin, bitterness, unforgiveness, pride, occult entanglements, lust, compromise. It gives spiritual backbone.

And this is crucial: many believers want deliverance from demons while refusing deliverance from flesh. But real strength begins with submission.

"Therefore submit to God. Resist the devil and he will flee from you." (James 4:7, NKJV)

Grace strengthens submission—and submission strengthens resistance.

4) Strengthening Grace Works Through the Word of His Grace

Weak believers are often Word-starved believers.

"So now, brethren, I commend you... to the word of His grace, which is able to build you up..." (Acts 20:32, NKJV)

The Word builds the inner man. It renews the mind. It sharpens discernment. It strengthens faith. It gives weapons for temptation. When the Word is neglected, strength drains quietly.

Strengthening grace often looks like a believer becoming consistent in Scripture—until the Word becomes bone and fire, not decoration.

5) Strengthening Grace Produces Quick Repentance and a Clean Conscience

A weak believer delays repentance. A strengthened believer repents quickly—because he fears God and loves holiness.

"Looking carefully lest anyone fall short of the grace of God..."
(Hebrews 12:15, NKJV)

Grace strengthens you to stay clean, not to stay comfortable. It makes you hate drifting. It makes you run back to God fast when you stumble.

6) Closing Exhortation: Receive Strength Like Bread, Not Like a Trophy

Strengthening grace is not a medal for the strong—it is bread for the needy.

If you feel weak, do not hide. Draw near.

If you feel tempted, do not delay. Cry out.

If you feel weary, do not drift. Return to the Word.

Because the God of all grace does not mock weakness—He supplies strength.

Closing Scriptures for Meditation (NKJV)

*   *(1 Peter 5:10)*

*   *(2 Corinthians 12:9)*

*   *(1 Corinthians 15:10)*

*   *(Acts 20:32)*

*   *(James 4:7)*

Settled by Grace — Unshakable Stability of Heart, Quiet Confidence in God, and Peace That Guards Against Drift

"But may the God of all grace… after you have suffered a while… settle you." (1 Peter 5:10, NKJV)

Many believers are saved, yet not settled. They are loved by God, yet restless inside. They are forgiven, yet anxious. They are sincere, yet unstable—tossed by emotions, shaken by people, moved by trends, disturbed by delay, rocked by trials.

Settling grace is one of the deepest works of God: He makes the believer steady. Not numb. Not passive. But anchored—quietly firm, spiritually grounded, inwardly stable.

This is grace that brings the soul into a mature rest—where storms may rage outside, but Christ reigns inside.

1) Settling Grace Comes After "You Have Suffered a While"

Suffering often creates one of two outcomes:

*   bitterness and instability

- or maturity and settledness

The difference is grace received with humility and fear of God.

"But may the God of all grace... after you have suffered a while..." (1 Peter 5:10, NKJV)

God uses "a while" to teach the heart that He is faithful. Settled believers are not those who never suffered. Settled believers are those who suffered and learned God personally—not as theology only, but as reality.

2) Settling Grace Anchors Identity So You Stop Living on Human Approval

Many believers are internally unstable because they are externally dependent—dependent on praise, affirmation, recognition, acceptance.

But when grace settles you, your identity becomes anchored in Christ. You stop needing constant validation. You stop living for applause. You begin living before God's face.

"Do not be haughty, but fear." (Romans 11:20, NKJV)

Godly fear settles the soul because it shifts the center: God becomes weightier than man. And when God is weightier, the heart becomes stable.

3) Settling Grace Produces Peace That Guards the Inner Man

Settled grace is not the absence of battle—it is the presence of divine guarding.

"And the peace of God, which surpasses all understanding, will guard your hearts and minds through Christ Jesus." (Philippians 4:7, NKJV)

This peace is not denial. It is a guard. It keeps anxiety from ruling. It keeps fear from driving decisions. It keeps the heart from being tossed.

This is why settled grace is intricately linked to prayerful living. The believer who never draws near will struggle to remain settled.

4) Settling Grace Stabilizes Doctrine So Deception Doesn't Move You

Some instability is emotional, but some instability is doctrinal. When believers are not grounded, they chase "new revelations," strange teachings, and counterfeit grace.

Settled grace makes the believer anchored in the Word—so he stops being easily impressed and becomes discerning.

"So now, brethren... the word of His grace... able to build you up..." *(Acts 20:32, NKJV)*

A settled believer is not easily shaken by end-times deception because he is anchored to Scripture and governed by the fear of the Lord.

5) Settling Grace Quietly Breaks Double-Mindedness

Many believers are unsettled because they are double-minded—two loyalties, two loves, two masters: Christ and self, holiness and secret sin, heaven, and the world.

Settling grace brings the heart into singleness.

"Draw near to God and He will draw near to you. Cleanse your hands... and purify your hearts, you double-minded." (James 4:8, NKJV)

When God settles you, He purifies the heart's divided places. He makes you whole. And wholeness produces stability.

6) Closing Exhortation: Let Grace Make You Steady Until You Become a Pillar

Beloved, the Lord is not only saving you—He is making you a pillar. A witness. A stable son or daughter in an unstable generation.

Let grace settle your heart.

Let grace anchor your mind.

Let grace quiet the storms inside.

Let grace make you firm in truth, firm in holiness, firm in love.

Because the God of all grace is able—after you have suffered a while—to make you unshakable.

Closing Scriptures for Meditation (NKJV)

*   *(1 Peter 5:10)*

*   *(Philippians 4:7)*

*   *(James 4:8)*

*   *(Acts 20:32)*

*   *(Romans 11:20)*

A Heart-Piercing Exhortation to the Reader

Beloved, do not waste your suffering. Do not let pain make you bitter. Let grace use it.

Let God perfect you—so hidden immaturity doesn't destroy you later.

Let God establish you—so you stop drifting in circles.

Let God strengthen you—so you stand against darkness without compromise.

Let God settle you—so your soul becomes quiet and firm in Christ.

Because the God of all grace is not only trying to get you through the storm. He is trying to make you into someone who can carry His glory after the storm.

And notice who does the work: "the God of all grace."

Not "some grace." Not "barely enough grace." All grace—every kind of grace needed for every stage of the journey.

CHAPTER TWENTY-ONE: THE THRONE OF GRACE — BOLD ACCESS, HOLY HELP, AND THE MERCY THAT CALLS THE BELIEVER TO STAY CLEAN

If grace is unquenchable, then the throne of grace is the fountainhead. It is the place where heaven's mercy is not a theory but a living invitation. It is where the believer learns that God is not only Judge—He is Father. Not only holy—He is merciful. Not only exalted—He is near.

But this throne is not casual. It is not a couch for spiritual laziness. It is a throne—meaning authority, kingship, rule. And it is a throne of grace—meaning the King rules His people by mercy and help, not by condemnation.

This chapter is meant to restore both confidence and godly fear: confidence to draw near, and fear to never treat mercy lightly.

"Let us therefore come boldly to the throne of grace, that we may obtain mercy and find grace to help in time of need." (Hebrews 4:16, NKJV)

1) "Let Us Therefore" — The Throne Is Open Because of Christ

Hebrews does not call us to boldness because we are good. It calls us to boldness because Jesus is our High Priest.

The throne of grace is open because blood has been offered, because sin has been judged in Christ, because reconciliation has been made, because the veil has been torn.

So, when you come, you are not coming as a beggar trying to convince God to love you. You are coming as one invited by covenant—because Christ has made a way.

This is why shame is such a weapon of darkness. Shame tries to keep you away from the very place where grace is supplied. But Hebrews commands the opposite: come.

2) "Come Boldly" — Confidence Without Presumption

Boldness is not arrogance. Boldness is not entitlement. Boldness is not casualness. Boldness is covenant confidence: God said I may come, therefore I will come.

Many believers stay weak because they only come to God when they feel worthy. But Hebrews teaches that the throne of grace is precisely where the unworthy obtain mercy and find help.

Yet we must guard this: boldness is not presumption. Presumption says, "God must accept my sin." Boldness says, "God will forgive my sin as I repent and draw near."

So, the throne produces two things at once:

- confidence to approach

- reverence to repent

3) "That We May Obtain Mercy" — Mercy for the Guilty, Mercy for the Weak

The first thing mentioned is mercy. Mercy is not merely comfort; mercy is God withholding the judgment we deserve. Mercy is what the guilty need. Mercy is what the weak need. Mercy is what the tempted need.

The throne of grace is where the believer obtains mercy:

- mercy after stumbling

- mercy under accusation

- mercy when the conscience is burdened

- mercy when the heart is broken

- mercy when the soul is weary

This mercy is not permission to continue in sin. It is rescue from sin's guilt and its power.

And here is the wonder: God does not ration mercy like man. He gives mercy generously to the repentant.

4) "Find Grace to Help" — Not Only Pardon, but Power

Then Hebrews says we "find grace to help." This is where many believers misunderstand grace. They think grace is only forgiveness. But this verse reveals grace as help—practical divine supply.

Grace to help means:

- grace to resist temptation before you fall

- grace to endure suffering without bitterness

- grace to obey when the flesh wants compromise

- grace to forgive when your emotions resist

- grace to stand in warfare

- grace to remain faithful in waiting

- grace to persevere to the end

This is why the throne is essential: because the Christian life cannot be lived on yesterday's help. Grace is a living supply.

The believer must learn to come often.

5) "In Time of Need" — Grace Is Timely, Specific, and Present

Grace is not only general; it is timely. "In time of need" means when the pressure is real, when the temptation is near, when the situation is urgent, when strength is low—that is the time to come.

The tragedy is that many come late. They come after compromise. They come after they have already fed the flesh. But Hebrews is teaching the believer to come before the fall—when the need first appears.

If you feel temptation rising, that is "time of need."

If you feel bitterness forming, that is "time of need."

If you feel weariness draining you, that is "time of need."

If you feel deception pulling at your mind, that is "time of need."

The throne of grace is a place of preventative mercy.

6) The Throne of Grace and Godly Fear: Help Is Given for Holiness, Not for Excuses

Here is where we must go deeper: the throne of grace is not a place where sin is made small. It is a place where sin is dealt with seriously and mercy is offered fully.

If a believer comes to the throne while intending to keep sin, he is not coming rightly. The throne is for those who want help to depart from evil.

Grace at the throne trains, corrects, empowers, and strengthens—because the King is holy.

This is why Hebrews also warns elsewhere about insulting the Spirit of grace (Hebrews 10:29). The throne is not mocked. Mercy is not to be despised.

So, the throne produces godly fear: you begin to tremble at the thought of treating holy mercy as common.

7) The Throne of Grace Is Where Perfecting, Strengthening, and Settling Grace Are Received

Now connect this directly to 1 Peter 5:10:

- Perfected by grace — the throne is where God mends the inner man through repentance, correction, and healing.

- Strengthened by grace — the throne is where God supplies power for obedience and endurance.

- Settled by grace — the throne is where peace guards the heart and stabilizes the soul.

A believer who avoids the throne will remain unperfected, weak, and unsettled. But a believer who comes often is built quietly into maturity.

8) How to Live as a Throne-of-Grace Believer (Practical Holy Habits)

1. Come daily, not only when you fail — grace is supply, not only cleanup.

2. Come honestly — no masks, no pretending; God sees anyway.

3. Come repentant — willing to forsake what God confronts.

4. Come believing — not doubting God's mercy in Christ.

5. Come quickly — delay hardens the heart.

6. Come with Scripture — bring the Word into prayer; let the Word shape your asking.

7. Come for help to obey — ask for strength before temptation conquers.

This is how the believer learns to live in unquenchable grace without abusing it.

Closing Exhortation: Come Boldly, but Come Holy

Beloved, the throne of grace is your refuge—yet it is also your training ground. It is where God forgives, yes—but also where God forms. It is where God comforts, yes—but also where God corrects. It is where God helps, yes—but also where God keeps you from drifting.

So do not stay away because of shame.

Do not come casually because of presumption.

Come boldly—because Christ opened the way.

Come humbly—because the King is holy.

Come often—because grace is supply.

Come repentant—because mercy is not to be despised.

And you will obtain mercy and find grace to help—right on time.

Closing Scriptures for Meditation (NKJV)

- *"Let us therefore come boldly to the throne of grace..." (Hebrews 4:16)*

- *"...that we may obtain mercy and find grace to help in time of need." (Hebrews 4:16)*

- *"May the God of all grace... perfect, establish, strengthen, and settle you." (1 Peter 5:10)*

CHAPTER TWENTY-TWO: TIME FOR GRACE — THE DAY OF VISITATION, THE DANGER OF DELAY, AND THE MERCY THAT MUST NOT BE DESPISED

There is a time when God calls.

A time when the Spirit convicts.

A time when the door is open.

A time when mercy is extended.

A time when grace is near.

And there is also a danger that most people do not fear enough: the danger of delay. Not because God is unwilling, but because the human heart can harden. Not because grace runs out, but because conscience can be seared. Not because God stops speaking, but because people stop listening.

This is why the Bible speaks about time in connection with salvation and grace. Grace is unquenchable, yes—but the Scriptures warn us not to treat grace like an endless postponement.

"Behold, now is the accepted time; behold, now is the day of salvation."
(2 Corinthians 6:2, NKJV)

The Spirit did not say "tomorrow." He said now.

1) The Mercy of God Has a "Now" — Grace Is Offered in the Present

Many believers and unbelievers alike live in the illusion of "later." Later I will repent. Later I will pray. Later I will get serious. Later I will forgive. Later I will obey. Later I will break that hidden sin. Later I will return.

But Scripture confronts that illusion. Grace calls in the present.

"Today, if you will hear His voice, do not harden your hearts…"
(Hebrews 3:15, NKJV)

Grace speaks as "today." Because "tomorrow" is not guaranteed, and the heart is not neutral when we delay. Every delay does something to the inner man.

Delay does not keep you the same.

Delay moves you somewhere—either toward surrender or toward hardness.

2) The Most Dangerous Word in Spiritual Life: "Later"

Let's go deeper: the devil does not need to convince most people to never repent. He only needs to convince them to delay repentance.

Delay is the enemy's quiet victory. It is how hearts become numb while still hearing truth. It is how people sit under preaching for years and remain unchanged. It is how conviction is felt and then ignored—until conviction becomes faint, and then rare, and then almost absent.

This is how many "fall short of the grace of God" (Hebrews 12:15)—not with open rebellion, but with slow postponement.

And once the heart hardens, sin begins to feel normal.

3) Grace Has Seasons of Visitation: When God Comes Near in Special Mercy

Scripture reveals that God visits. He draws near. He convicts. He awakens. He opens the door of repentance. He sends truth. He sends warnings. He sends mercy.

When Jesus wept over Jerusalem, He revealed something sobering: they missed their moment.

"...because you did not know the time of your visitation." (Luke 19:44, NKJV)

That means there was a time they should have recognized. A time of mercy. A time of grace. A time to repent. A time to receive the Messiah. But they missed it—and judgment followed.

This should produce godly fear. Not fear that God is cruel, but fear that hearts can become blind even while God is calling.

4) What Happens When People Despise "Time for Grace"

Paul warns:

"Or do you despise the riches of His goodness, forbearance, and longsuffering, not knowing that the goodness of God leads you to

repentance?" (Romans 2:4, NKJV)

God's goodness is meant to lead you to repentance, not to comfort you in sin. God's patience is meant to bring you to surrender, not to make you casual.

But when a person despises grace-time, something frightening begins:

- conviction becomes weaker

- sin becomes easier

- repentance feels unnecessary

- compromise feels "understandable"

- prayer becomes delayed

- the Word becomes dull

- the fear of God fades

- the heart becomes hardened

This is not because God changed, but because the heart hardened.

5) "After You Have Suffered a While" — Grace Uses Time to Perfect, Not to Excuse

Now connect this to 1 Peter 5:10. God uses time wisely.

Some believers interpret "a while" as abandonment. But God is using time to form something deep:

- perfecting grace (mending)

- establishing grace (rooting)

- strengthening grace (empowering)

- settling grace (stabilizing)

However, the same time that perfects the humble can harden the proud. The same delay that matures the obedient can corrupt the careless.

Time does not automatically bless you. Time exposes you.

Grace makes time fruitful—if you yield.

6) Time for Grace in the Believer: The Urgency of Repentance

This is not only for unbelievers. Believers must also honor the time of grace—especially when conviction comes.

When the Spirit convicts you about:

- unforgiveness

- lust

- dishonesty

- bitterness

- pride

- compromise

- idolatry

- prayerlessness

- spiritual laziness

- secret sin

…that is your time for grace. That is the moment to come to the throne, to repent, to cut it off, to return.

Because delayed repentance is not harmless. It is dangerous.

"Looking carefully lest anyone fall short of the grace of God…"

(Hebrews 12:15, NKJV)

Falling short often begins with ignoring small convictions.

7) Time for Grace and the Fear of the Lord: "Do Not Harden Your Hearts"

Hebrews repeats the warning for a reason:

"Today, if you will hear His voice, do not harden your hearts…"
(Hebrews 3:15, NKJV)

Hardness is a spiritual condition where truth no longer penetrates. It is when the Word hits the ear but not the conscience. It is when sin is tolerated with little fear. It is when grace is spoken about but no longer treasured.

Godly fear is the opposite of hardness. Godly fear says:

- *"Lord, I will not delay."*

- *"Lord, I will not excuse."*

- *"Lord, keep my heart tender."*

- *"Lord, I respond while You are speaking."*

8) How to Recognize Your "Time for Grace" (Signs God Is Visiting)

You may be in a time of grace when:

- the Word pierces you unusually

- conviction comes repeatedly about the same matter

- God sends confirmations through Scripture, preaching, and counsel

- you feel a holy urgency to repent

- sin begins to feel heavy and repulsive

- you sense God calling you deeper in prayer

- doors close that were feeding your flesh

- you feel stirred toward holiness and sobriety

These are not random emotions. These are often the Spirit's visitation—God drawing you.

Do not resist it.

9) Practical Response: What to Do When You Sense Time for Grace

1. Come to the throne immediately (Hebrews 4:16)

2. Confess honestly (1 John 1:9)

3. Forsake what God exposes (cut off the source)

4. Forgive quickly (do not let bitterness root)

5. Return to the Word daily (the word of His grace builds you)

6. Seek accountability (especially for recurring sin)

7. Obey promptly (obedience seals the moment)

This is how grace-time becomes transformation, not merely emotion.

Closing Exhortation: Respond While Grace Is Calling

Beloved, do not gamble with "later." Do not treat patience like permission. Do not let the Spirit speak and you remain unchanged.

Now is the accepted time.

Today is the day to respond.

This is your moment to repent.

This is your time to return.

This is your time to draw near.

This is your time to obey.

Because grace is unquenchable—but hearts can become hardened. And the fear of the Lord is wisdom: respond while God is speaking.

Closing Scriptures for Meditation (NKJV)

- *"Behold, now is the accepted time; behold, now is the day of salvation." (2 Corinthians 6:2)*

- *"Today, if you will hear His voice, do not harden your hearts..." (Hebrews 3:15)*

- *"...because you did not know the time of your visitation." (Luke 19:44)*

- *"Or do you despise the riches of His goodness...?" (Romans 2:4)*

- *"Looking carefully lest anyone fall short of the grace of God..." (Hebrews 12:15)*

CHAPTER TWENTY-THREE:
GRACE FOR GRACE — EVER-INCREASING SUPPLY, FRESH MEASURES OF MERCY, AND THE CALL TO DEEPER HOLINESS

There is grace that begins your walk with God—saving grace.

There is grace that sustains you—keeping grace.

There is grace that trains you—sanctifying grace.

There is grace that strengthens you—warfare grace.

But then Scripture opens a door into something even deeper—grace for grace: grace upon grace, grace replacing grace, new measures of divine supply as you continue in Christ. Grace not as a one-time gift, but as an ever-flowing river.

"And of His fullness we have all received, and grace for grace." (John 1:16, NKJV)

This is not a poetic decoration. This is a spiritual reality. John is describing life in Christ: the believer does not receive a small portion and then survive by his own strength. The believer receives from Christ's fullness—and that fullness supplies grace in layers, seasons, and fresh measures.

But here is where godly fear must guard the truth: greater grace calls for greater surrender. When God gives more, He expects more. When grace increases, accountability increases. "Grace for grace" is not an invitation to spiritual laziness; it is a call to deeper consecration.

1) "Of His Fullness" — Grace Comes from a Person, Not a Concept

John does not say "of a doctrine we have received." He says:

"Of His fullness we have all received..." (John 1:16, NKJV)

Grace is not merely a message. Grace is not merely a principle. Grace flows from Christ Himself. He is full—full of truth, full of life, full of mercy, full of power, full of holiness, full of love. And the believer receives from Him.

This means: when you are depleted, you do not merely need motivation. You need Christ's fullness again. When you are tempted, you do not merely need discipline; you need fresh grace from the fullness of Jesus. When you are weary, you do not merely need rest; you need renewal from Him.

Grace is personal. It is received by abiding.

2) What Does "Grace for Grace" Mean?

(Going Deeper into the Phrase Itself)

The phrase carries a powerful idea: grace in exchange for grace—grace replacing grace, wave after wave, fresh supply after fresh supply.

Like this:

- yesterday's grace carried you yesterday

- today's grace is offered today

- tomorrow's grace will be given tomorrow

Not because yesterday's grace was insufficient, but because God is continually supplying what is needed in each moment.

This is why believers cannot live on memories alone. Past encounters are precious, but present grace is necessary. The manna principle still applies spiritually: you gather daily.

So "grace for grace" means the Christian life is meant to be lived in continual reception—continual drawing near—continual dependence.

3) Grace for Grace in Seasons: God Gives Specific Grace for Specific Needs

There are graces for different seasons:

- grace to repent

- grace to forgive

- grace to endure waiting

- grace to stand in warfare

- grace to resist temptation

- grace to suffer without bitterness

- grace to obey when it costs you

- grace to minister when you feel empty

- grace to lead when you feel inadequate

- grace to heal and restore when wounds are deep

This is why the throne of grace matters (Hebrews 4:16). It is the place where "grace for grace" becomes practical. God does not just give grace "generally." He gives grace "to help in time of need."

So, when the need changes, the grace comes in new measure.

4) "Grace for Grace" Is Not Mere Comfort — It Is Fresh Supply for Holiness

Many want fresh grace for comfort, but not fresh grace for holiness. But grace for grace is supply for sanctification.

The more you receive from His fullness, the more His fullness reshapes you. You receive mercy—then you receive strength. You receive forgiveness—then you receive discipline. You receive comfort—then you receive correction. You receive help—then you receive training.

This is how God keeps grace from becoming cheap: every fresh grace comes with deeper transformation.

"For the grace of God... teaching us that, denying ungodliness..."
(Titus 2:11–12, NKJV)

Grace trains. If grace is increasing, then training is increasing. God is not merely helping you survive; He is forming Christ in you.

5) The Danger: Receiving "Grace for Grace" in Vain

Here is the sobering side: it is possible to receive grace repeatedly and still remain unchanged if the heart refuses surrender.

"We then, as workers together with Him also plead with you not to receive the grace of God in vain." (2 Corinthians 6:1, NKJV)

Receiving grace "in vain" means grace came—but the life did not yield. Mercy was offered—but repentance was delayed. Conviction came—but sin was kept. Help was available—but the heart stayed stubborn.

Godly fear must guard "grace for grace" because the more grace you receive, the greater the guilt if you despise it.

Grace is not only kindness; it is holy opportunity.

6) Grace for Grace Produces a Life of Continual Repentance and Continual Renewal

A believer living in "grace for grace" becomes quick to repent and quick to return. They don't drift long. They don't defend sin. They don't tolerate spiritual dullness. They know where the supply is, and they return often.

They become like a branch that keeps drawing sap from the vine. Not sometimes—continually.

When grace becomes continual, repentance becomes normal—not as condemnation, but as cleansing. Not as despair, but as renewal.

7) Grace for Grace and Godly Fear: More Grace Means More Stewardship

This is a crucial revelation: greater grace is greater stewardship.

When God increases grace:

- you cannot remain casual

- you cannot remain double-minded

- you cannot keep secret sin

- you cannot live on yesterday's devotion

- you cannot treat holiness as optional

Greater grace is not merely "more blessing." It is more light. And more light means greater accountability.

Jesus taught this principle: greater revelation requires greater response. So "grace for grace" should make the believer tremble—in gratitude and reverence.

8) How to Walk Daily in "Grace for Grace" (Practical Spiritual Posture)

1. Abide in Christ — make intimacy central, not occasional.

2. Come to the throne early — before temptation grows.

3. Stay in the Word — the word of His grace builds you up.

4. Obey promptly — delayed obedience blocks fresh supply.

5. Repent quickly — keep the conscience clean.

6. Stay thankful — thanksgiving protects from entitlement.

7. Walk in godly fear — reverence keeps grace precious.

This is how grace becomes a river, not a memory.

Closing Exhortation: Receive from His Fullness, and Let Grace Increase Your Holiness

Beloved, Christ is full. His fullness does not diminish. His supply does not run out. And of His fullness we have received—grace for grace.

So do not live as a spiritual orphan.

Do not live as a believer running on fumes.

Do not live as though yesterday's grace is all you have.

Come again. Receive again. Draw near again.

And as grace increases, let surrender increase.

As mercy increases, let holiness increase.

As help increases, let obedience increase.

Because "grace for grace" is God's way of carrying you from beginning to end—until you stand in glory.

Closing Scriptures for Meditation (NKJV)

- *"Of His fullness we have all received, and grace for grace." (John 1:16)*

- *"...find grace to help in time of need." (Hebrews 4:16)*

- *"...not to receive the grace of God in vain." (2 Corinthians 6:1)*

- *"The grace of God... teaching us..." (Titus 2:11–12)*

CHAPTER TWENTY-FOUR: GRACE AND MERCY — MERCY WITHHOLDS JUDGMENT, GRACE IMPARTS POWER, AND BOTH LEAD TO REPENTANCE

Many believers speak of grace and mercy as if they are the same thing. They are closely related, but they are not identical. Understanding the difference is not a minor doctrine—it protects the soul from deception.

Because when mercy is misunderstood, people grow careless.

And when grace is misunderstood, people remain bound.

Mercy answers the question: What does God do with my guilt?

Grace answers the question: What does God do with my weakness?

Mercy withholds what we deserve.

Grace supplies what we do not deserve.

And both are meant to lead the believer not into comfort only, but into repentance, holiness, and godly fear.

1) Mercy: God Not Giving the Judgment We Deserve

Mercy is God's compassion toward the guilty and the miserable. Mercy is God restraining judgment. Mercy is the holy kindness of God that does not treat us according to our sins when we repent and come to Him.

It is mercy that causes God to forgive.

It is mercy that rescues the repentant from wrath.

It is mercy that lifts the fallen.

Paul speaks of this mercy clearly:

"...not by works of righteousness which we have done, but according to His mercy He saved us..." (Titus 3:5, NKJV)

Notice: salvation is tied to mercy. Without mercy, there is no salvation. Without mercy, guilt would condemn us. Without mercy, the law would crush us.

Mercy is the reason you are not consumed.

2) Grace: God Giving the Help and Power We Do Not Deserve

Grace is more than forgiveness. Grace is divine help—power given to the undeserving to live in a new way.

Grace is God's strength for obedience.

Grace is God's supply for endurance.

Grace is God's training for holiness.

Grace is God's empowerment for service.

This is why Hebrews says:

"...find grace to help in time of need." (Hebrews 4:16, NKJV)

Grace helps. Grace strengthens. Grace empowers.

So, mercy cancels condemnation—grace breaks bondage.

3) Mercy and Grace Together: The Two Hands of God Saving a Sinner

Here is the picture:

- Mercy removes the sentence.

- Grace changes the life.

Mercy says, "I will not punish you as your sins deserve."

Grace says, "I will empower you to no longer live as you used to."

This is why true salvation never stops at mercy. It continues into grace.

A person who only wants mercy wants to avoid punishment.

A person who receives grace wants to become holy.

Grace and mercy together create a life of transformation.

4) The Goodness of God: Mercy and Grace Lead to Repentance, Not Presumption

Paul issues a warning that is needed in this generation:

"Or do you despise the riches of His goodness, forbearance, and longsuffering... not knowing that the goodness of God leads you to

repentance?" (Romans 2:4, NKJV)

What is "goodness" here? It includes mercy and grace. And the purpose of that goodness is repentance. Not laziness. Not delay. Not "once saved always saved no matter how I live." The goodness of God leads to a changed heart.

So, when a believer receives mercy but refuses repentance, he is despising mercy.

When a believer claims grace but refuses holiness, he is abusing grace.

Mercy and grace are not cushions for sin. They are God's rescue from sin.

5) Mercy Without Grace Produces People Who Are Forgiven But Still Enslaved

Many Christians live in a cycle:

- sin

- guilt

- confession

- relief

- repeat

They experience mercy often, but they do not walk in the power of grace. They keep returning to the same bondage because they want forgiveness without transformation.

But grace exists to break the cycle.

"For sin shall not have dominion over you, for you are not under law but under grace." (Romans 6:14, NKJV)

If sin still dominates, the believer must come deeper into grace—not merely to be forgiven again, but to be empowered to walk free.

This is why grace, and mercy must be preached together. Mercy alone comforts; grace transforms.

6) Grace Without Mercy Becomes Harsh Religion

Now the other danger: some preach "power" and "holiness" without mercy. That produces condemnation, not transformation. That produces fear without love. That produces religion.

But Scripture never separates holiness from mercy. God is holy, and He is compassionate. God disciplines, and He restores. God corrects, and He forgives.

So, the believer must never become harsh toward others while claiming holiness. The one who has received mercy must show mercy.

"Blessed are the merciful, for they shall obtain mercy." (Matthew 5:7, NKJV)

Mercy produces humility. Mercy makes you gentle. Mercy reminds you who you would be without Christ.

7) Mercy and Grace in Warfare: Mercy Restores, Grace Strengthens

This is deeply practical:

- When you fall, mercy lifts you back up.

- When you are tempted, grace strengthens you to resist.

- When you are accused, mercy assures you of forgiveness in Christ.

- When you are weak, grace supplies power.

- When you are weary, mercy comforts you and grace carries you.

Mercy is the refuge.

Grace is the power.

And both flow from the throne.

8) Godly Fear: The More Mercy You Receive, the More You Must Tremble at Despising It

Here is the sobering truth: mercy is precious; therefore, mercy is dangerous to despise. The more God has forgiven you, the more fearful it should make you to return to the same darkness.

Not fear that God hates you—fear that you could trample what is holy.

This is why Hebrews warns about insulting the Spirit of grace (Hebrews 10:29). Mercy and grace are holy gifts. To use them as excuses is to become spiritually reckless.

The right response to mercy is gratitude and repentance.

The right response to grace is obedience and holiness.

9) Living Daily Under Mercy and Grace (Practical Posture)

1. Come to the throne daily (Hebrews 4:16)

2. Confess quickly (1 John 1:9)

3. Ask for power to obey (grace to help)

4. Keep a tender conscience (fear of the Lord)

5. Show mercy to others (forgive as you were forgiven)

6. Do not delay repentance (time for grace is now)

7. Stay in Scripture (the word of His grace builds you up)

This is how mercy and grace become a living walk, not a religious phrase.

Closing Exhortation: Don't Choose One—Receive Both

Beloved, you need mercy when you are guilty.

And you need grace when you are weak.

Mercy forgives you.

Grace changes you.

Mercy restores you.

Grace establishes you.

Mercy comforts you.

Grace strengthens you.

So come boldly to the throne of grace—obtain mercy, and find grace to help—so your life is not only forgiven but transformed.

Closing Scriptures for Meditation (NKJV)

- *"...according to His mercy He saved us..." (Titus 3:5)*

- *"Let us... come boldly... obtain mercy and find grace to help..." (Hebrews 4:16)*

- *"For sin shall not have dominion over you... under grace." (Romans 6:14)*

- *"The goodness of God leads you to repentance..." (Romans 2:4)*

Chapter Twenty-Five: Grace and Peace — Peace With God, Peace Within, and the Sobering Truth That Peace Cannot Fellowship With Willful Sin

Grace and peace are often paired in Scripture like a holy greeting, but they are not mere religious words. They reveal a divine order:

Grace is the source. Peace is the fruit.

Grace is what God gives. Peace is what God produces.

Grace reconciles. Peace settles.

Grace saves. Peace guards.

This is why the apostles repeatedly wrote:

"Grace to you and peace..." (see many epistles, NKJV)

They were not being poetic. They were declaring a spiritual reality: where grace is received rightly, peace is produced genuinely.

But here is where we must go deeper with godly fear: there is a false peace that comes from ignoring conviction, and a true peace that comes from being right with God. The Church must learn to discern the difference—because many have called numbness "peace" while living in compromise.

1) Peace Begins With Grace: Peace With God Comes Through the Gospel

The deepest peace is not emotional calm; it is reconciliation with God. Before Christ, humanity is not neutral toward God—we were separated by sin. Grace is what bridges that separation.

Grace brings justification, and justification brings peace.

"Therefore, having been justified by faith, we have peace with God through our Lord Jesus Christ." (Romans 5:1, NKJV)

Peace with God is not earned by human goodness; it is received through Christ. The cross ends hostility. The blood ends enmity. Grace makes peace possible.

So, the first meaning of "grace and peace" is this: God's grace brings you into peace with Him.

2) Peace Within: Grace Produces the Peace of God That Guards the Heart

Once peace with God is established, God also gives the peace of God—the inner guarding, stabilizing peace that protects the mind and heart.

194

"And the peace of God, which surpasses all understanding, will guard your hearts and minds through Christ Jesus." (Philippians 4:7, NKJV)

This is not a shallow calm. This is a guarding force. It restrains anxiety. It quiets inner turbulence. It keeps the believer from being tossed by fear and circumstances.

But notice: this peace guards "through Christ Jesus." That means peace is maintained by staying near to Christ—by abiding, by prayer, by obedience, by trust.

Grace brings you in. Grace keeps you near. And peace is produced.

3) Grace and Peace Are Not Separated: Where Grace Trains, Peace Settles

Grace does more than forgive—it trains you to live godly (Titus 2:11–12). And as grace trains you out of sin and into holiness, peace increases.

This is why many believers have no peace while claiming grace: they want mercy but resist training. They want comfort but refuse repentance. They want peace but keep the very thing that destroys peace—willful sin.

True peace flourishes where the conscience is clean.

A conscience that is constantly violated will become troubled, numb, or deceptive—but it cannot remain truly peaceful before God.

4) The Sobering Truth: Peace Cannot Fellowship With Willful Sin

Here we must speak plainly: peace is not compatible with rebellion.

God may still love a believer who is compromising, but that believer will lose the sweetness of peace and the stability of joy—because sin brings inner conflict. Sin grieves the Spirit. Sin clouds the mind. Sin defiles the conscience. Sin opens doors to accusation and fear.

The believer may still say "peace, peace," but Scripture warns against false assurances.

The peace of God is a guardian that keeps the heart stable, but if the believer insists on darkness, he will silence conviction—and what remains is not peace; it is spiritual numbness.

That is dangerous.

This is why godly fear is essential: fear keeps peace pure. Fear keeps the conscience tender. Fear keeps the believer from calling compromise "peace."

5) Grace Produces Peace Through Repentance: Peace Returns When the Heart Returns

One of the great mercies of God is that peace can return quickly when repentance is sincere. The throne of grace is not only a place of mercy; it is a place of restoration.

When a believer confesses, forsakes, and returns, peace returns—not as a reward, but as a result of reconciliation and cleansing.

"If we confess our sins, He is faithful and just to forgive us… and to cleanse us…" (1 John 1:9, NKJV)

Cleansing restores clarity. Clarity restores confidence. Confidence restores peace.

This is why delayed repentance is dangerous: it prolongs inner turmoil and increases hardness.

6) Grace and Peace in Warfare: Peace Is Not Weakness— Peace Is Stability Under Attack

Peace is not the absence of battle; it is stability in battle. Peace is the believer standing firm while hell rages, because the soul is anchored in Christ.

This is why Scripture calls it "the gospel of peace" as part of the armor (Ephesians 6:15). Peace is part of warfare. It keeps the believer from panic. It keeps the believer from rash decisions. It keeps the believer from fear-driven compromise.

Grace gives this peace—not as sedation, but as strength.

A peaceful believer is often a dangerous believer to darkness—because fear cannot manipulate him.

7) Grace and Peace Spread: Peaceful Believers Become Peacemakers

Grace and peace are not only for personal comfort; they overflow into relationships. A believer living in grace and peace becomes less reactive, less offended, less argumentative, less harsh.

Because the peace of God governs the heart, the believer stops being controlled by wounds and begins to walk in forgiveness.

And this is also a test: many claim grace but are constantly divisive. Many claim peace but are constantly bitter. Where grace is truly reigning, peace begins to rule.

8) How to Walk Daily in Grace and Peace (Practical)

1. Return to the throne daily (Hebrews 4:16)

2. Live repentant (keep the conscience clean)

3. Stay in the Word (the word of His grace builds you up)

4. Pray instead of panic (Philippians 4:6–7)

5. Forgive quickly (bitterness steals peace)

6. Reject willful sin (sin robs peace)

7. Walk in godly fear (fear keeps peace pure)

Closing Exhortation: Let Grace Rule So Peace Can Guard

Beloved, grace is not only meant to save you—it is meant to reign in you. And when grace reigns, peace guards. When mercy restores, peace returns. When holiness grows, peace deepens. When obedience becomes consistent, peace becomes stable.

Do not settle for false peace that comes from ignoring conviction.

Seek true peace—the peace that flows from grace received in repentance, obedience, and faith.

Grace and peace are not slogans. They are a life.

Closing Scriptures for Meditation (NKJV)

- *"Having been justified by faith, we have peace with God..."* *(Romans 5:1)*

- *"The peace of God... will guard your hearts and minds..."* *(Philippians 4:7)*

- *"Be anxious for nothing... and the peace of God..."* *(Philippians 4:6–7)*

- *"If we confess our sins... cleanse us..."* *(1 John 1:9)*

CHAPTER TWENTY-SIX: GROWING IN GRACE — INCREASING IN CHRIST'S FULLNESS, DEEPENING IN HOLINESS, AND MATURING UNDER THE FEAR OF THE LORD

Grace is not only how you begin—it is how you continue. Grace is not only the doorway into salvation—it is the pathway into maturity. And Scripture makes this a command, not a suggestion:

"But grow in the grace and knowledge of our Lord and Savior Jesus Christ..." (2 Peter 3:18, NKJV)

If the Spirit commands growth, then staying stagnant is dangerous. A believer who does not grow does not stay the same—he drifts. He becomes vulnerable to deception, temptation, and hardness. That is why this chapter must go deeper: growing in grace is one of the greatest protections God gives the believer in the last days.

But we must define it correctly. Growing in grace does not mean growing in looseness, casualness, or permissiveness. True grace grows you into holiness, sobriety, and Christlikeness.

Grace grows where the fear of the Lord is honored.

1) What It Means to Grow in Grace: Not Just More Comfort—More Christ

Many think growing in grace means feeling more accepted. Yes, the believer should grow in assurance and confidence in Christ. But if that confidence does not also produce transformation, it becomes false security.

To grow in grace means:

- your love for holiness increases

- your hatred for sin increases

- your conscience becomes more tender

- your repentance becomes quicker

- your faith becomes steadier

- your discernment becomes sharper

- your obedience becomes more consistent

- your intimacy with Christ becomes deeper

- your dependence on the Spirit becomes greater

In other words: more Christ, less self.

Growing in grace is Christ forming Himself in you.

2) Grace Grows Where Humility Lives

Scripture gives a direct law of the kingdom:

"God resists the proud, but gives grace to the humble." (James 4:6, NKJV)

If grace is given to the humble, then growth in grace requires growth in humility. Pride blocks increase. Pride argues with correction. Pride justifies sin. Pride seeks recognition. Pride resists repentance. Pride may be religious, but it is dry.

But humility attracts grace like rain attracts thirsty ground. The humble believer learns quickly, repents quickly, forgives quickly, obeys quickly. And because of that, he grows.

So, the first question of growing in grace is not, "How gifted am I?" It is, "How humble am I?"

3) Grace Grows Through the Word of His Grace

A believer cannot grow in grace while starving the soul of Scripture.

"So now, brethren, I commend you... to the word of His grace, which is able to build you up..." (Acts 20:32, NKJV)

The Word builds you up—this is growth language. The Word renews the mind. The Word exposes deception. The Word trains the heart. The Word strengthens faith. The Word keeps the conscience alive.

Many who "stop growing" did not stop believing—they stopped feeding. And when feeding stops, growth stops. And when growth stops, vulnerability increases.

Grace grows where the Word is treasured.

4) Grace Grows Through Obedience, Not Mere Information

There are believers who know much but grow little. They collect sermons, notes, and verses but remain unchanged. Why? Because grace grows not merely through hearing, but through obeying.

Jesus said:

"If you know these things, blessed are you if you do them." (John 13:17, NKJV)

Obedience is where grace becomes muscle. Obedience is where truth becomes life. Obedience is where maturity forms.

Grace is not only a teacher (Titus 2:11–12); it is also an empowerment to obey what it teaches. When the believer obeys, grace increases—not as wages, but as capacity. Obedience enlarges the vessel for more grace.

5) Grace Grows Through Repentance: Tenderness Is a Sign of Increase

Here is a deep mark of growth: as you grow in grace, you become quicker to repent and more sensitive to sin.

Not more condemned—more sensitive. Not more hopeless—more responsive.

A believer growing in grace cannot sit comfortably in sin. The Spirit will not allow it. Conviction becomes sharper, not weaker. The fear of the Lord becomes stronger, not smaller.

This is why false grace is exposed: false grace produces numbness. True grace produces tenderness.

"Today, if you will hear His voice, do not harden your hearts..."
(Hebrews 3:15, NKJV)

Growth in grace means the heart becomes softer over time, not harder.

6) Grace Grows Through Suffering: "After You Have Suffered a While"

Many want growth without trials, but Scripture ties maturity to endurance. And 1 Peter 5:10 reveals it clearly:

"...after you have suffered a while, perfect, establish, strengthen, and settle you." (1 Peter 5:10, NKJV)

Grace grows through suffering because suffering purifies motives. It breaks reliance on flesh. It reveals idols. It strengthens perseverance. It deepens prayer. It makes heaven more real than earth.

But only if the believer yields. If he complains and hardens, suffering can make him bitter. But if he comes to the throne and stays humble, suffering becomes a furnace where grace increases.

7) Growing in Grace Requires Growing in the Fear of the Lord

Growth in grace is not growth away from fear; it is growth into reverence.

Why? Because the more you understand mercy, the more you tremble at despising it.

"Do not be haughty, but fear." (Romans 11:20, NKJV)

Fear here is not terror; it is reverence that keeps you from drifting into presumption. It is the fear that says, "Lord, keep me. I do not want to fall short. I do not want to insult the Spirit of grace."

A believer growing in grace becomes more watchful, not more careless.

8) Signs You Are Growing in Grace (A Spiritual Mirror)

You are growing in grace when:

- you crave Scripture more than entertainment

- you repent faster and excuse sin less

- you forgive more quickly and hold less offense

- you endure trials with less complaining

- you are less driven by man's approval

- you are more sensitive to the Spirit's convictions

- you are more patient in waiting

- you are more stable in doctrine

- you are more thankful, less entitled

- you are more humble, more teachable

These are not personality changes. These are grace increases.

9) The Warning: Stagnation Is Dangerous

This command is urgent because stagnation is not safe. A stagnant believer becomes easy prey:

- deception begins to sound right

- temptation begins to feel normal

- prayer begins to feel optional

- holiness begins to feel extreme

- conviction begins to fade

- "later" becomes the language

That is why "growing in grace" is not optional—it is survival for the remnant.

Closing Exhortation: Grow Until Christ Is Seen

Beloved, do not measure your life merely by gifts, activity, or church attendance. Measure your life by growth in grace—growth in holiness, repentance, humility, and intimacy with Christ.

Grace is unquenchable, but you must continue to receive it. You must continue to draw near. You must continue to abide. You must continue to obey.

Grow in grace until you become steady.

Grow in grace until your conscience is clean.

Grow in grace until temptation loses its voice.

Grow in grace until prayer becomes breath.

Grow in grace until Christ is formed in you.

To Him be the glory—both now and forever.

Closing Scriptures for Meditation (NKJV)

- *"But grow in the grace and knowledge of our Lord..." (2 Peter 3:18)*

- *"God resists the proud, but gives grace to the humble." (James 4:6)*

- *"...the word of His grace... able to build you up..." (Acts 20:32)*

- *"...after you have suffered a while... perfect... strengthen... settle..." (1 Peter 5:10)*

- *"Do not be haughty, but fear." (Romans 11:20)*

CHAPTER TWENTY-SEVEN: AMAZING GRACE — THE WONDER THAT SAVES THE WORST, SUSTAINS THE WEAK, AND PRODUCES TREMBLING GRATITUDE

We say the words "Amazing Grace" so often that many have forgotten what they mean.

For some, it has become a song title.

For others, it is a phrase used to soften sin.

For many, it is sentimental language—beautiful, but not feared.

But grace is truly amazing, not because it makes sin small, but because it reveals a Savior so great that He can rescue the worst without becoming stained by their darkness. Grace is amazing because it does what no human religion can do: it takes the condemned and justifies them, takes the enslaved and frees them, takes the filthy and cleanses them, takes the broken and restores them, takes the rebellious and transforms them into sons and daughters.

Grace is amazing because it is holy mercy poured out at infinite cost.

And if you truly see it, you will not treat it casually—you will tremble.

1) Amazing Grace Begins With the Truth About Us: We Were Lost, Not Slightly Off

Grace is only amazing when you understand what you were saved from.

Scripture does not say humanity was "mostly good." It says humanity was lost. Dead in sin. Separated from God. Under judgment.

"And you He made alive, who were dead in trespasses and sins..." *(Ephesians 2:1, NKJV)*

Dead people do not rescue themselves. Lost people do not find the way by themselves. This is why grace is amazing: it is God coming to the helpless.

Grace is not God helping good people become better. Grace is God rescuing dead people and giving them life.

2) Amazing Grace Is Christ Entering Our Condition to Lift Us Out

The wonder is not only that God forgave. The wonder is that God came near—through Christ—to bear our judgment and break our chains.

"But we see Jesus... that He, by the grace of God, might taste death for everyone." *(Hebrews 2:9, NKJV)*

Grace did not remain in heaven as an idea. Grace appeared in flesh.

Grace walked among sinners. Grace touched lepers. Grace ate with outcasts. Grace confronted hypocrites. Grace carried a cross. Grace tasted death.

Grace is amazing because it is not cheap. It is blood-purchased.

3) Amazing Grace Justifies the Ungodly — Without Calling Ungodliness Acceptable

This is the heart of the gospel: God justifies sinners who believe, not because sin is acceptable, but because Christ paid.

"...that having been justified by His grace we should become heirs..."
(Titus 3:7, NKJV)

Justified means declared righteous—not by works, but by Christ's righteousness credited to the believer by faith.

This is amazing.

But it must be said with godly fear: justification is not permission to remain ungodly. It is the legal door that brings the believer into a new life.

Grace justifies—and then grace sanctifies.

4) Amazing Grace Is Not Only Forgiveness — It Is Divine Training

Many want grace as pardon but resist grace as training. Yet Titus 2 reveals that the same grace that also saves trains:

"For the grace of God... has appeared... teaching us that, denying ungodliness and worldly lusts, we should live soberly, righteously, and godly..." (Titus 2:11–12, NKJV)

Amazing grace does not only wash you; it teaches you.

It does not only lift you; it trains you.

It does not only forgive you; it changes you.

So, if grace has not changed your relationship with sin, you have not yet understood grace. Because grace is not an excuse—it is a teacher.

5) Amazing Grace Is God's Patience With Weak People — Yet It Does Not Celebrate Weakness

Grace is amazing because God is patient. He bears with our immaturity. He corrects without discarding. He restores when we repent. He strengthens when we are weak.

"But may the God of all grace... perfect, establish, strengthen, and settle you." (1 Peter 5:10, NKJV)

Yet grace does not celebrate weakness as identity. It strengthens weakness into endurance. It perfects immaturity into maturity. It settles instability into steadiness.

Amazing grace does not leave you as you were.

6) Amazing Grace Produces Thanksgiving — Not Entitlement

Paul reveals what happens when grace spreads:

"...that grace... may cause thanksgiving to abound to the glory of God." (2 Corinthians 4:15, NKJV)

The proof that grace is understood is not pride. It is gratitude. It is thanksgiving. It is worship.

When grace is understood, entitlement dies. Complaining decreases. Humility increases. The heart becomes soft again. The believer becomes thankful not only for blessings, but for mercy.

An unthankful believer has forgotten grace.

7) Amazing Grace and Godly Fear: The Deeper the Mercy, the Deeper the Reverence

This is where we must pierce the heart: the more you see what grace cost, the more you fear despising it.

A believer who can sin casually while saying "amazing grace" has not truly seen the cross.

Because grace is amazing—and therefore grace is holy.

The cross is mercy—but it is also judgment. God judged sin in Christ. So how can we take lightly what God judged so severely?

This is why Romans 2:4 is so serious:

"...not knowing that the goodness of God leads you to repentance?"
(Romans 2:4, NKJV)

The goodness is meant to lead to repentance, not to delay. And when repentance is delayed, grace is despised.

So amazing grace should produce a holy fear:

- fear of grieving the Spirit

- fear of returning to bondage

- fear of treating holy blood as common

- fear of falling short through neglect

- fear of unbelief growing quietly

Not fear that God is cruel—fear that God is holy.

8) The Test of Amazing Grace: Does It Make You Love Holiness?

Here is a simple spiritual mirror:

If grace is amazing to you, holiness becomes precious to you.

Grace makes you hate what nailed Jesus to the cross.

Grace makes you flee what dishonors the One who saved you.

Grace makes you love correction because you love God.

Grace makes you sensitive to conviction.

Grace makes you eager to obey.

Amazing grace does not produce a careless Christian. It produces a reverent disciple.

Closing Exhortation: Never Let "Amazing Grace" Become Common Words

Beloved, do not let familiarity steal wonder. Do not let repetition remove fear. Do not let a song title replace revelation.

Grace is amazing because Christ is amazing.

Grace is amazing because the cross is real.

Grace is amazing because mercy triumphed over judgment for the repentant.

Grace is amazing because God did not leave us lost.

So let grace remain amazing—by living in repentance, holiness, thanksgiving, and godly fear.

Let your life prove that grace is not only sung—it is obeyed.

Closing Scriptures for Meditation (NKJV)

- *"...by the grace of God, might taste death for everyone." (Hebrews 2:9)*

- *"...justified by His grace..." (Titus 3:7)*

- *"The grace of God... teaching us..." (Titus 2:11–12)*

- *"...grace... may cause thanksgiving to abound..." (2 Corinthians 4:15)*

- *"But may the God of all grace... perfect... strengthen... settle..." (1 Peter 5:10)*

TO THE HEART OF GRACE: THE UNQUENCHABLE MERCY OF GOD IN CHRIST — THE LOVE THAT SAVES, THE LIGHT THAT TRAINS, AND THE FIRE THAT KEEPS US HOLY

As we begin to "land the plane," we must come to the center of it all—because if grace is treated as a topic only, the reader may admire it and still miss it. But if grace is seen as the very heartbeat of God revealed in Jesus Christ, then grace will not remain a chapter—it will become a holy encounter.

Grace is not merely God being nice.

Grace is not God lowering His standards.

Grace is not God ignoring sin.

Grace is God rescuing sinners at the cost of His Son, and then raising them into a life that matches heaven.

Grace is God's love moving toward the undeserving…

and God's holiness moving into the redeemed.

1) The Heart of Grace Is a Person: Jesus Christ

Grace is not a mist in the air. Grace has a face. Grace has hands that were pierced. Grace has a voice that calls sinners by name. Grace is Jesus.

"And of His fullness we have all received, and grace for grace." (John 1:16, NKJV)

You do not merely "learn grace." You receive grace from His fullness. That means grace is relational: it is received through abiding, surrender, and drawing near—repeatedly.

2) The Heart of Grace Is This: God Comes to You Before You Could Ever Reach Him

This is what destroys pride and produces worship. You were not saved because you climbed high enough. You were saved because God came low enough.

"For by grace you have been saved through faith, and that not of yourselves; it is the gift of God…" (Ephesians 2:8, NKJV)

Grace is God's initiative. God's pursuit. God's gift.

And when the heart sees this, boasting dies.

3) Grace Is Not Only Forgiveness — It Is Divine Training

This is where many stop too early. They want grace as a blanket, but not grace as a teacher. Yet the Spirit places the center of grace right here:

"For the grace of God that brings salvation has appeared to all men, teaching us that, denying ungodliness and worldly lusts, we should live soberly, righteously, and godly in the present age..." (Titus 2:11–12, NKJV)

The heart of grace is holy instruction.

Grace does not only pardon the sinner—grace trains the saint.

If grace is truly received, it produces a new relationship with sin: not friendship, not negotiation, but warfare and separation.

4) Grace Leads to Repentance — Not Delay

Grace is not meant to make you comfortable in what kills you. Grace is meant to call you out.

"...not knowing that the goodness of God leads you to repentance?" (Romans 2:4, NKJV)

This is one of the clearest windows into the heart of grace: God's kindness is not permission—it is invitation. Grace is God saying, "Come home. Come clean. Come into the light."

That is why "time for grace" matters. When grace speaks, delaying is dangerous—not because God is stingy, but because the heart can harden.

5) Grace Is Help in the Moment of Need

Grace is not only for beginnings. Grace is for battle. For weakness. For temptation. For suffering. For endurance. For daily life.

"Let us therefore come boldly to the throne of grace, that we may obtain mercy and find grace to help in time of need." (Hebrews 4:16, NKJV)

The heart of grace is that God does not merely command—He supplies.

He does not merely demand holiness—He provides help to walk in it.

So, grace is not "try harder." Grace is "draw nearer."

6) Grace Is God Completing What Trials Expose

This is where grace becomes deeply personal. Suffering often reveals what still needs healing, maturing, and strengthening. And God does not waste your pain.

"But may the God of all grace... after you have suffered a while, perfect, establish, strengthen, and settle you." (1 Peter 5:10, NKJV)

The heart of grace is that God is not only saving you from hell—He is saving you from collapse. From drift. From deception. From hidden fractures that would destroy you later.

Grace finishes what God started.

7) The Heart of Grace Produces Godly Fear, Not Carelessness

Here is the holy paradox: the more grace you truly see, the more you fear despising it.

Not a fear that runs from God—but a fear that clings to Him.

Not terror—but reverence.

Not condemnation—but sobriety.

Because when grace is understood, sin becomes heavier, not lighter—since the cross reveals what sin costs.

So, grace does not make the believer casual. It makes the believer grateful and watchful.

8) The Heart of Grace Is Love with Fire in It

Some preach grace without holiness—people become lawless.

Some preach holiness without grace—people become crushed.

But the heart of grace is God's love that purifies. Love that rescues and then refines. Love that forgives and then transforms.

Grace is love that will not leave you chained.

A Soft Landing for the Soul

Beloved, if this book leaves the reader with anything, let it be this:

- Grace is not merely what God does for you; it is what God does in you.

- Grace is not merely a covering; it is a calling.

- Grace is not only a gift; it is a government—Christ reigning in the heart.

- Grace is not permission to continue; it is power to change.

So, the right response to grace is not only "thank You."

It is also "change me."

Not only "forgive me."

But also "keep me."

Not only "save me."

But also "sanctify me."

Closing Prayer

Father, God of all grace, I come to the throne of grace in the name of Jesus Christ. Let Your grace not only forgive me, but teach me. Let Your mercy not only restore me, but cleanse me. Deliver me from receiving grace in vain. Keep my heart tender. Put the fear of the Lord within me—so I do not take holy things lightly. Perfect what is lacking in me. Establish me in truth. Strengthen me against temptation. Settle my soul in Your peace. And let my life prove that Your grace is truly unquenchable. In Jesus' name, amen.

FINAL CHAPTER: UNQUENCHABLE GRACE — STAY PERFECTED, ESTABLISHED, STRENGTHENED, AND SETTLED UNTIL YOU STAND IN GLORY

Beloved reader, if you have walked with me through these chapters, then you already know this: grace is not a soft word meant to make sin feel small. Grace is a holy power meant to make Christ feel weighty.

Grace is God's mercy reaching down to rescue you—yes.

But grace is also God's hand staying on you to keep you.

Because the same grace that saves must also sustain.

And the same grace that forgives must also form.

And the same grace that opens the door must also keep you walking on the narrow way.

This is why the Spirit did not end our journey with comfort only. He ended it with a fourfold promise and a fourfold call:

"But may the God of all grace… after you have suffered a while, perfect, establish, strengthen, and settle you." (1 Peter 5:10, NKJV)

This is not merely a blessing to quote. It is a pathway to live. It is God's intention for you until the end.

So, hear this final chapter like a trumpet in the spirit—gentle enough to heal, strong enough to awaken.

1) Stay Perfected by Grace — Do Not Resist God's Inner Work

There is a grace that forgives you, and there is a grace that mends you.

Perfecting grace is God repairing what you hide, maturing what you excuse, cleansing what you tolerate, restoring what trials exposed. Perfecting grace is Christ refusing to leave you half-formed.

Beloved, do not resist the hand that is healing you.

Do not defend what God is confronting.

Do not protect what God is trying to purge.

Do not call conviction "negativity."

Do not silence the Spirit because truth is uncomfortable.

Because every time you ignore conviction, you do not remain neutral—you harden. And hardened hearts do not drift into holiness; they drift into deception.

So, stay perfected:

- stay repentant

- stay teachable

- stay soft

- stay honest before God

Let grace finish what God started. Do not carry fractures into your next season. Let the God of all grace mend you completely.

2) Stay Established by Grace — Refuse to Drift

Believers do not fall overnight. They drift.

Drift is subtle. Drift looks like less prayer. Less Scripture. Less tenderness. More entertainment. More compromise. More rationalizing. More "later." Less fear of God.

This is why Paul commended believers to "the word of His grace" because it builds you up (Acts 20:32, NKJV). The Word establishes you. It roots you. It strengthens your doctrine. It keeps your conscience awake.

Beloved, if you want to be established:

- stay in the Word until the Word lives in you

- stay in fellowship instead of isolation

- stay accountable instead of hidden

- stay sober instead of spiritually casual

You were not saved to be unstable. You were saved to be steadfast.

And hear this with godly fear: if you do not hold fast to truth, the age will disciple you instead. The world will catechize your mind. The flesh will train your appetites. And you will wonder how you became weak.

So, stay established.

3) Stay Strengthened by Grace — Do Not Fight with Empty Hands

There is no Christian life without warfare. Even if you avoid the language of battle, battle will still find you: temptation, pressure, accusation, trials, spiritual oppression, deception.

But you were never meant to fight with willpower alone.

Strength is a grace.

"My grace is sufficient for you..." (2 Corinthians 12:9, NKJV)

Strengthening grace is God empowering obedience in the moment of pressure—so you do not fall into sin "because you were weak." Weakness is not your excuse; weakness is your invitation to draw near.

Do not wait until the temptation becomes a flame before you run to the throne. The throne of grace is where strength is supplied in time of need (Hebrews 4:16, NKJV)—which means when need rises, you run.

So, stay strengthened:

- stay prayerful before temptation grows

- stay watchful when weariness increases

- stay filled when the flesh tries to rule

- stay armed with Scripture

- stay submitted to God

- stay resistant to the devil

Because a strengthened believer is not one who never feels pressure— he is one who keeps standing under pressure.

4) Stay Settled by Grace — Let God Quiet the Storms Within

Many believers are saved but not settled. They live forgiven but anxious. Accepted but restless. Loved but unstable. They are tossed by people's opinions, shaken by delay, disturbed by trials, pulled by emotions.

But settling grace is God making your soul steady.

Not numb. Not passive. Steady.

Settled grace is when the believer no longer lives from panic, but from peace. When the mind is anchored in truth. When identity is rooted in Christ. When the heart is no longer easily moved by offense. When the believer becomes a pillar.

Beloved, God can settle you—after you have suffered a while—so that your pain does not produce bitterness, and your waiting does not produce unbelief.

So, stay settled:

- stay thankful instead of entitled

- stay forgiving instead of bitter

- stay humble instead of proud

- stay near the throne instead of far away

- stay in peace instead of panic

The peace of God is not for perfect circumstances; it is for surrendered hearts.

5) A Final Warning in Love: Do Not Receive Grace in Vain

This is the line in the sand:

Grace can be received outwardly and still be resisted inwardly.

Grace can be heard and still be despised.

Grace can be preached and still be taken for granted.

"We… plead with you not to receive the grace of God in vain." (2 Corinthians 6:1, NKJV)

Grace is vain when you keep your sin.

Grace is vain when you delay repentance.

Grace is vain when you silence conviction.

Grace is vain when you trade holiness for comfort.

Grace is vain when you keep "peace" while living in rebellion.

Beloved, do not let your story become tragedy. Do not let mercy be wasted. Do not let patience become your excuse.

Now is the accepted time. Today is the day to respond (2 Corinthians 6:2, NKJV).

6) The Call of This Book: Return to the Throne Until You Finish Well

If there is one practical command that will keep you perfected, established, strengthened, and settled, it is this:

Keep coming to the throne of grace.

Not once. Not occasionally. Continually.

Come when you are weak.

Come when you are tempted.

Come when you fall.

Come when you're weary.

Come when you don't feel worthy.

Come when you feel proud.

Come when you feel numb.

Come when you feel afraid.

The throne is not only where you obtain mercy—it is where you find grace to help. It is where God trains you into holiness. It is where the God of all grace keeps your heart alive.

FINAL EXHORTATION

Let Grace Make You a Witness, Not a Warning

Beloved reader, heaven is not looking for believers who can speak of grace while living in compromise. Heaven is looking for believers who are living proof that grace is real.

Let your life preach:

- grace that forgives

- grace that trains

- grace that strengthens

- grace that keeps

- grace that makes you holy

- grace that finishes the race

Let your testimony be this: not that you were perfect in yourself, but that the God of all grace perfected you. Not that you were strong in yourself, but that the God of all grace strengthened you. Not that you were stable by personality, but that the God of all grace settled you.

And when you stand before the Lord, let it be said: you finished well.

FINAL PRAYER

Father, God of all grace, I come before You in the name of Jesus Christ. I confess that without Your grace I cannot stand. Keep me from receiving grace in vain. Perfect what is lacking in me. Establish me in Your truth. Strengthen me against temptation and every work of darkness. Settle my heart in Your peace. Put Your fear within me so I do not take Your mercy lightly. Teach me to come boldly to the throne of grace daily—until I finish my race and stand in Your eternal glory. In Jesus' name, amen.

CLOSING REFLECTION & COMMITMENT

Unquenchable Grace — A Personal Response to the God of All Grace

Take a quiet moment. Breathe. Let the words you have read settle into your spirit. This is not a page to rush. This is a holy pause—between what you have learned and what you will live.

"But may the God of all grace... perfect, establish, strengthen, and settle you." (1 Peter 5:10, NKJV)

Grace has spoken to you through these chapters. Now grace is calling for your response.

1) REFLECTION: LET YOUR HEART ANSWER HONESTLY

A. On Perfecting Grace

- What areas of my life still feel "unhealed," "unfinished," or "fractured"?

- Have I been resisting conviction, correction, or repentance in any area?

- Is there a sin I have been excusing instead of forsaking?

- What is one thing the Lord has been repeatedly dealing with me about?

Write it here:

B. On Establishing Grace

- Where am I most unstable spiritually—prayer, the Word, obedience, consistency?

- What distractions have been weakening my devotion to Christ?

- Have I drifted into spiritual laziness, isolation, or compromise?

- What practical change must I make to become rooted?

Write it here:

C. On Strengthening Grace

- Where do I feel most weak—temptation, fear, discouragement, weariness, doubt?

- Do I run to the throne before I fall—or only after?

- What pattern of temptation has been repeatedly battling me?

- What does "grace to help in time of need" look like for me daily?

Write it here:

D. On Settling Grace

- What has been stealing my peace—bitterness, anxiety, offense, comparison, control?

- Is my heart restless because I am double-minded in any area?

- Have I been carrying unresolved pain that needs surrender to

God?

- What would a "settled soul" look like in my daily life?

Write it here:

2) COMMITMENT: A COVENANT PRAYER BEFORE GOD

(Read slowly. Make it personal. Mean it.)

Father, God of all grace, I come to You in the name of Jesus Christ. I thank You for saving me by grace and calling me to Your eternal glory. I confess that I cannot live this life in my own strength.

Today, I make a holy commitment before You:

I COMMIT TO BE PERFECTED BY GRACE

Lord, search my heart. Expose what is hidden. Heal what is broken. Correct what is crooked. I renounce every excuse I have used to justify sin. I choose repentance. I choose humility. I surrender to Your perfecting work in me.

I COMMIT TO BE ESTABLISHED BY GRACE

Lord, keep me from drifting. Root me in Your Word. Establish my faith and doctrine. Deliver me from spiritual laziness, compromise, and double-mindedness. Teach me to be consistent in prayer and Scripture, and faithful in the secret place.

I COMMIT TO BE STRENGTHENED BY GRACE

Lord, strengthen me where I am weak. Give me grace to resist temptation and stand against darkness. Teach me to run to the throne in time of need—not after I fall, but before. Let Your strength be made perfect in my weakness.

I COMMIT TO BE SETTLED BY GRACE

Lord, settle my heart in Your peace. Deliver me from anxiety, offense, bitterness, and inner turbulence. Anchor my identity in Christ. Make me steady, sober, and unshakable in this generation.

Father, keep me from receiving Your grace in vain. Put Your fear within me—so I do not take holy things lightly. Help me to continue in Your goodness. Help me to endure. Help me to finish well.

I declare that Jesus Christ is my Lord. I belong to You. I choose holiness. I choose obedience. I choose the narrow way. And I choose to come boldly to the throne of grace daily—until the end.

In Jesus' name, amen.

3) PERSONAL VOWS (WRITE YOUR OWN WORDS)

Lord, by Your grace, I will…

1.

2.

3.

4) A SIMPLE DAILY RULE OF LIFE (7-DAY START)

To help your commitment become a lifestyle, commit to these for the next 7 days:

- Daily Word: Read at least one chapter of Scripture each day.

- Daily Throne: Come to the throne of grace in prayer morning and night.

- Daily Repentance: Confess quickly—do not carry guilt or compromise.

- Daily Watchfulness: Identify one temptation trigger and cut it off.

- Daily Thanksgiving: Write three things you thank God for each day.

5) SIGN & DATE (A MARKER OF SINCERITY)

Name: ____

Date: ____

Scripture Commitment:

"But may the God of all grace... perfect, establish, strengthen, and settle you." (1 Peter 5:10, NKJV)

BENEDICTION

May the God of all grace—who has called you to His eternal glory by Christ Jesus—keep you under the covering of the blood and the power of His Spirit. May He perfect what is lacking in you, establish you firmly in His truth, strengthen you against every work of darkness, and settle your heart in His unshakable peace. May the fear of the Lord preserve you, and may the Word of His grace build you up until your life becomes living proof that His grace is truly unquenchable.

And now, may you go forward in humility and holy confidence—coming boldly to the throne of grace to obtain mercy and find grace to help in every time of need. May your love for Jesus deepen, your obedience remain steady, your conscience stay tender, and your faith endure to the end—until the day you stand in His presence with joy. In the name of our Lord and Savior Jesus Christ, amen.